100 answers to 100 questions

ask · discover · live smart

about Prayer

100 answers to 100 questions

ask · discover · live smart

about

Prayer

Christian
LIFE
A STRANG COMPANY

Most CHRISTIAN LIFE products are available at special quantity discounts for bulk purchase for sales promotions, premiums, fund-raising, and educational needs. For details, write Christian Life, 600 Rinehart Road, Lake Mary, Florida 32746, or telephone (407) 333-0600.

100 Answers to 100 Questions About Prayer

Published by Christian Life
A Strang Company
600 Rinehart Road
Lake Mary, Florida 32746

www.strang.com

Cover design by Whisner Design Group, Tulsa, Oklahoma

ISBN 10:   1-59979-274-5
ISBN 13:   978-1-59979-274-3

BISAC Category: Religion/Christian Life/Prayer

First Edition

08 09 10 11 12—9 8 7 6 5 4 3 2 1

Printed in the United States of America

Proceed with much prayer,
and your way will be made plain.

John Wesley

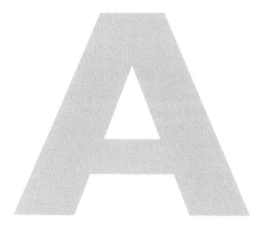

Contents

Introduction 12

The Purpose of Prayer

1. How do you define prayer? 14
2. Why does God want you to pray? . . . 16
3. Should you pray when you are
   uncertain God even hears you? 18
4. How can you talk to someone
   you cannot see? 20
5. Is prayer as complicated as it
   sounds? 22
6. Does fate or prayer determine
   your life? 25
7. What is "talking to God"? 27
8. Can you pray without knowing
   the Bible? 29
9. Does God *need* you to pray? 31

Does Prayer Make a Difference?

10. Will God do what He wants
    anyway? 33
11. Is prayer just to make you feel
    better about life? 35
12. If you are happy, why pray? 37
13. If someone is praying for you, is it
    enough to help? 39
14. How do you know if God hears
    your prayer? 41
15. Do the prayers of one person
    matter in the world? 43
16. Does God care about your
    opinions on situations? 46
17. Do prayers for big world issues
    make a difference? 48

18. What if others are praying about
    an issue in a different way than you? 50

19. Does prayer change the future? 52

Learning to Pray

20. How do you learn to pray? 54

21. Is there a format to use in prayer? . . . 56

22. Is formal language necessary when
    praying? 58

23. Whom do you pray to—God, Jesus,
    or the Holy Spirit? 60

24. Is it all right to sometimes pray
    in different ways? 62

25. How do you know whom to
    pray for? 64

26. Do you have to pray in the
    morning? 67

27. How often should you pray? 69

28. Can you just tell God how
    you feel? 71

29. Do you have to pray aloud? 73

Types of Prayer

30. Why is it important to include
    praise to God? 75

31. Is thankfulness an important part
    of prayer? 77

32. What does it mean to pray a
    blessing on someone? 79

33. How do you tell God what you
    and others need? 81

34. How do you pray the words of
    the Bible? 83

35. What is the Lord's Prayer? 85

36. Is it enough to say only the
    Lord's Prayer daily? 88

37. Can you write down your prayers
    to God? 90

38. Should part of prayer be listening,
    not talking? 92

39. How can you pray when you have
    no words left? 94

40. Can a song be a prayer to God? 96

Things That Hamper Prayer

41. Does it matter if you forget to
    pray every day? 98

42. Can you pray when you know you
    are doing wrong? 100

43. Must you have right motives
    when you pray? 102

44. Does God hear when you have
    not forgiven someone? 104

45. Can you pray if you are not sure
    you believe? 106

46. Should you pray when you do
    not feel like it? 109

47. How do you overcome feeling God
    will not help you? 111

48. Can you pray if you do not feel
    close to God? 113

49. Does it matter if you are in church
    when you pray? 115

Answers to Prayer (or Not)

50. What do you do if there is
    no answer? 117

51. Do you lack faith if you ask God
    more than once? 119

52. How do you know what God
    is saying? 121

53. In what ways are prayers for direction answered? 123

54. How long do you keep praying? ... 125

55. How can you continue to pray for someone? 127

56. If there is no answer, did God say no? 130

57. What if you do not like the answer God gives? 132

58. Can you have a conversation with God? 134

59. Does God speak only through the Bible? 136

How to Pray God's Will

60. How do you know to pray what God wants? 138

61. Is there a way to know what to pray? 140

62. What happens if you pray the wrong way? 142

63. How do you know when to stop praying for someone? 144

64. What if the Bible does not give an example of prayer for your situation? 146

65. Is it wrong to pray for what you think should happen? 148

66. How do you know if your prayers are selfish? 151

67. Can you pray with others if you don't agree on how to pray? 153

Praying for Others

68. Doesn't the Bible say to pray in secret? 155

69. How do you pray for people who are sick? 157

70. How do you know what God wants for the sick and suffering? . . . 159

71. How do you pray for very complicated situations? 161

72. What's a good way to remember whom to pray for? 163

73. Should you pray for your pastor? . . 165

74. Do you need to pray for politicians and leaders? 167

75. How do you pray for someone to come to faith in God? 169

76. How can you pray for someone who has hurt you? 172

77. Does it do any good to pray for the poor? 174

78. How should you pray for your children? 176

79. Can you ask God to "fix" your spouse? 178

80. How can you pray for someone you don't know? 180

Praying for Yourself

81. Is it all right to ask for things? 182

82. What is there to pray for besides your needs? 184

83. Can you ask God for your purpose in life? 186

84. Should you bother God with small matters? 188

85. Can you pray to not go through hard times? 190

86. What do you pray when you aren't getting well? 193

87. Is it all right to ask God to change your traits or habits? 195

88. Is it enough to ask only once for forgiveness? 197

89. How do you pray when it is hard to forgive? 199

90. How can you pray for someone you don't like? 201

91. What do you pray when you do not need anything? 203

Power in Prayer

92. How can anyone pray continually? 205

93. Should you have high expectations of God in prayer? 207

94. Does it matter if you are doing what God wants? 209

95. How does the Holy Spirit help you pray? 211

96. Does fasting make prayer more effective? 214

97. How do you keep from getting discouraged? 216

98. What happens if you do not feel close to God? 218

99. Does love have anything to do with prayer? 220

100. What benefit comes from praying with others? 222

Introduction

One of life's biggest marvels is the mystery and power of prayer. Prayer holds the key to real connection to God, and provides the hope and solutions you need when faced with the difficulties of modern-day life.

Rather than something attainable only by holy men and women secluded from society, prayer is available to all. Prayer allows you to develop a close relationship with the God who created you. He welcomes your prayer and wants to meet your needs as you trust Him with your most precious thoughts and concerns.

This book provides answers to your questions about prayer and clarifies your role in conversation with God. You can find specific answers quickly, yet with the depth of understanding you need. You will find inspiration to guide your prayers in times of happiness and in times of grief. You will learn how your faith blooms when you spend time every day with God. You will see how to bring your needs to God, as well as how to pray for the needs of others.

Prayer serves not just as a means for securing the things you need, but also as a transforming and intimate connection to God. As your relationship with God grows and deepens, you will enjoy His company as you never expected, and your life will be increasingly changed for good.

Come, join in the prayer journey that will enrich your life and give you hope for the world to come.

What a privilege is ours:
the privilege of prayer!
Billy Graham

I chose you and appointed you that you
should go and bear fruit, and that
your fruit should remain, that
whatever you ask the Father in My
name He may give you.
John 15:16–17, NKJV

---

question

How do you define prayer?

Prayer, while familiar to many, can give the impression of being something mysterious, superstitious, or just for "religious" people. Most people remember bedtime or mealtime prayers memorized when they were young, but putting the practice of prayer into adult life takes a fresh look at what it means to pray to God. To make prayer a part of your daily life, you need to understand the reason for prayer, and better understand the One who calls you to pray.

answer

Intimate, real conversation with God, called prayer, is woven throughout the Bible. Men and women spoke to God, and the conversations recorded cover all aspects of human emotion and need, from anger to joy, and from thankfulness to intense need. Thomas Merton called prayer an expression of who people are, and described prayer as something that completes and fills people's emptiness.

God does ask people to pray regularly, and in addition, many examples of prayer written in the Bible model the incredible facets of prayer in the life of a Christian. At the most basic level, prayer lets you access God and enables you to call on His name for your cares and needs as well as others'. It is a way to ask God to act with His wisdom, mercy, and compassion in your family, your city, or your world.

Prayer allows you to spend time with God and show your devotion to Him in praise and thanks. As you spend more time in prayer and enjoy the presence of God more and more, you find yourself understanding the relationship Jesus described with the words "you are my friends" (John 15:15, NLT). Even if you find yourself drawn to God in a different way, you have the assurance that prayer is a journey and a progression, and that if you faithfully practice prayer, you will move closer and closer to God.

worth thinking about

▶ **No relationship** can grow and become deeper if you converse infrequently. Praying daily will bring you closer to God.

▶ **To be able** to speak freely to the One who created all that exists is an indescribable privilege. Realizing that can help you keep the best attitude about prayer and your relationship to God.

▶ **See prayer** as God's perfect plan for filling empty and lonely places with divine friendship.

> *Prayer is the contact of a living soul with God. In prayer, God stoops to kiss man, to bless man, and to assist man in everything that God can devise or man can need.*
>
> E. M. Bounds

question

Why does God want you to pray?

The Bible is clear when it says that people should pray, and that they should pray frequently. What is harder to grasp is why the almighty and all-knowing God of the universe would want the people He created to speak to Him every day in prayer. Because He knows everything, it is strange to think that He needs people to ask Him for anything. What could He need that you can provide?

answer

Luke 18:1 says Jesus told His disciples that "men always ought to pray and not lose heart" (NKJV). But why? Researchers continue to find more and more proof that there are physical and mental benefits of prayer, even when the subjects of research did not know someone was praying for them. From a strictly scientific standpoint, you can see that humans benefit in many ways from prayer in their lives.

God wants something from you through prayer that only you can provide. It is not something scientific or something routine. God wants a deep and intimate relationship with you. He wants you to speak to Him in prayer and for you to linger long enough to sense what He says to you. He wants that bond, that relationship, to be alive and growing as you spend time every day in that most precious conversation.

In reality, God does not need you to pray, but incredibly, He *wants* you to pray. Yes, if you pray, you will grow in your relationship with God, and you will be healthier, happier, and more secure in life. You will become more concerned about others, and you will pray more for them. Prayer develops the relationship you have with God to the point that He calls you "friend." From that point, praying for any other reason seems less important than knowing God in that way. And if you want to see God be God in your life and in the lives of others, you can ask Him to do that. Prayer changes things, and prayer changes you.

worth thinking about

▶ **Anyone feels** flattered when someone wants to enjoy time together with them. Now, picture the God of the entire universe wanting to spend time with you. Amazing.

▶ **Few things** in life are truly win-win situations. Prayer is an exception, for there is no way to lose by learning to pray and by making prayer a part of your life.

▶ **Knowing that you** give God pleasure by wanting to communicate with Him and grow closer to Him makes remembering to pray much easier.

> *We must not pray first of all because it feels good or helps, but because God loves us and wants our attention.*
> Henri Nouwen

question

▾

Should you pray when you are uncertain God even hears you?

Whether you are just beginning to practice prayer or you have prayed your whole life, you may sometimes battle the fear that God cannot be hearing you. Since you are most keenly aware of your end of the prayer conversation, you do not always have feedback that would help you know your prayers are heard. It may feel wrong to pray if you are not convinced that God is listening, and so the lingering question may keep you from actually petitioning God about the concerns you have in your life.

answer

▾

Lazarus was a friend of Jesus. There is a story in the Bible about Lazarus' becoming ill. Someone came to tell Jesus of the illness so that Jesus could simply speak the word and make Lazarus well. The messenger described Lazarus as the one Jesus loved, rather than as the one who loved Jesus. The strength of healing prayer lay not in Lazarus; rather, the strength of healing prayer lay in Jesus, who heard the prayer.

Good news! The pressure is off. Your level of belief is not what makes prayer effective. Honest, heartfelt prayer, even if expressing doubt, is prayer God hears and answers. He will prove Himself if you will just do your part. As you pray, and as you see God's answers to the prayers you have lifted to Him, your faith will grow.

It is also true that the Bible says many miss out on what they need because they do not ask. If you lack the confidence and faith that God hears every word you pray, then ask Him for that confidence and faith. Ask Him to increase the faith you have and convince you that He hears your prayers. Read what the Bible has to say about prayer and God's faithfulness. Make a concerted effort to let God change your mind about His ability to hear and to care for all that you find important.

worth thinking about

▶ **God would not** ask you to pray without ceasing if He was not planning on hearing your prayers and answering them.

▶ **Prayer is the lifeblood** of your faith walk. Make it a priority to ask God for help. Spend enough time in prayer to give God time to work.

▶ **If you read** about the lives of strong Christians throughout history, you will see the pattern of faith and answered prayers.

> *He attends to the prayer of the wretched. He won't dismiss their prayer.*
> Psalm 102:17, THE MESSAGE

question

4

How can you talk to someone you cannot see?

Depending on that which you can see or sense has been a part of your life since you were a baby. It is part of being human and living in a finite, three-dimensional world. So when you contemplate prayer, it is hard to imagine carrying on a conversation or a relationship with someone you cannot see. Grappling with that idea may hinder your prayers, or at least cause them to be too small or too timid to enjoy all that God has for you. What you want is to feel at ease with prayer.

answer

Faith does not depend on what you see, what you can prove, or what you can touch, and neither does prayer. Experience, however, makes the difference in praying with confidence. The more you exercise your faith, the more your faith will grow. The more you trust God to be who He is and to do what He promises, the more you will experience God. So how do you reach the place of praying with such confidence to God, whom you cannot see?

If you will press through the discomfort of speaking to God, you will find that spending time praying and investing time in reading the Bible will make you more and more comfortable with addressing God in prayer. A good way to learn to connect with God in a way that helps you focus on Him is to commit to thirty days of prayer. For one month, share with God from your heart, and praise Him for who He is and what He has done. Keep a journal or make notes to yourself about what you are doing and sensing. Stick with that month, no matter how you feel about praying.

Chances are you will see answers to specific prayers you prayed. You may feel a connection to God in much the same way you would feel a connection to a person you know well. Giving prayer a chance changes your life in some way. The thing God wants is your willingness to try. As with any relationship, your prayer journey with God will grow and change over time. God will help you meet those changes, and He will ensure that you will be blessed because of it.

worth thinking about

▶ As you begin to know God and know how He answers your prayers, you can see that prayer is not much different from talking to someone you love on the phone.

▶ Since you cannot imagine what God really looks like, you can concentrate on the quality of relationship you have with God, and your prayer will grow and mature.

▶ Look at creation and thank God for His marvels. The more you see that causes you to want to praise God, the closer you will feel to Him.

We live by faith, not by what we see.
2 Corinthians 5:7, CEV

5 question

Is prayer as complicated as it sounds?

Communication today is easier than ever before, but it's also more complicated because of the rapidly changing face of technology and equipment. You index and place your friends and family on certain plans, and calls must be made at only certain times of the day or night and not others. The guidelines you must remember are endless. It is easy to understand why prayer, too, may seem to be complicated. After all, prayer is communication.

answer

In prayer you speak directly to God, and He speaks to you. Prayer brings your cares, concerns, and thanks to Him. Just as two people who loved each other would speak in a language of everything from murmurs to longer conversations, God also wants a love relationship with you, fostered and supported by the language of prayer. God doesn't need to hear long elaborate prayers in any particular formula. He simply needs to hear words uttered from your heart to His.

Jesus taught His disciples not to use grand words and long repetitions when they prayed. He said that God knew what they needed before they even asked, so they were not required to ask in a certain way, to use a formula, or even to worry about what others thought about their prayers. He went so far as to tell His disciples to go and pray by themselves in their rooms, because their conversation was just for God to hear.

The same understanding of speaking to God applies to your own prayers. If you have a love relationship, you have the right to go to God and speak to Him with every concern and care that is on your mind. He wants to have a strong and growing relationship with you, and He wants to meet your needs and watch you grow and mature as a believer. The bottom line is simply this: God hears the cry of the heart.

worth thinking about

▶ **God gave prayer** to His people as a gift, and it is so straightforward that even children can pray freely and with great affection for God.

▶ **Simple words** can convey great thoughts or large concerns. Free yourself from the worry of which word to choose, and just speak to God as you would to a friend.

▶ **Wisdom sometimes** dictates fewer words and more times of silence. Be sensitive to times when less is more.

> *Prayer is simply talking to God. He speaks to us: we listen. We speak to Him: He listens. A two-way process: speaking and listening.*
>
> Mother Teresa

question

question

How do your personal prayers stack up against the prayers of saints?

answer

answer

On the same rock upon which all the saints rested their prayers I, too, rest mine. Moreover I pray for the same thing for which they all prayed; besides, I have just as great a need as did those great saints.

Martin Luther

6 question

Does fate or prayer determine your life?

The question of fate or prayer touches on a debate long held by seekers of spiritual matters. Is life mapped out by an unknown force called fate, or is a person's life mapped out unequivocally by God? If your life is mapped by God, is His will predetermined from the beginning, or does prayer make a difference in how this rolls out? The answer lies not in clear-cut black and white, but is in a balance of several truths.

answer

God has a plan for your life. That clear truth anchors your hope and confidence. "'I know the plans I have for you,' says the LORD. 'They are plans for good and not for disaster, to give you a future and a hope'" (Jeremiah 29:11 NLT). God wants good for you, and for the things in your life ultimately to move from chaos or suffering to a place where good springs out of the very things that caused you grief. What a comforting thought.

However, if you shrink back from prayer because it seems unnecessary, you are shortchanging God in the ultimate plan for your life. Fate does not have a death grip on your future. Prayer changes things, and prayer changes you. Praying brings you closer to God, and closer to what He wants for your life. Praying changes the lives of those around you. Prayer allows you to enjoy and delight in God.

You can stand in a place where you believe with all your heart that God's will and purposes will work good out of everything, and that He wants good for your life. That is a position you can depend on. And you can believe at the same time that in the vast wisdom of the God who gave His children choices, you can choose to pray with His help and make positive changes in yourself, other people, and situations around you.

worth thinking about

▶ **Ecclesiastes says** that there is a time for every purpose under heaven—a time to be born, a time to die. God knows all those times.

▶ **When you pray**, you are joining in with what God is doing in the world. You are agreeing with His will and higher purpose, and that brings God pleasure.

▶ **Just as God** knew your beginning, He knows the path your future will take. You have no reason to fear what is to come.

> *God does not want us to shrug our shoulders, shuffle our feet, and mutter "Que sera, sera, whatever will be, will be." On the contrary, Scripture makes it plain that we are involved with this life of ours—and the lives of others as well. Certain things simply will not happen . . . unless we pray.*
>
> Joni Eareckson Tada

7 question

What is "talking to God"?

Talking to God sounds too casual a way to address the God of the universe. You talk to others throughout your day without thinking much about it. Those conversations do not require you to study beforehand or carefully consider every statement. Surely prayer would seem to be more than just casual conversation with God. The thought crosses your mind that if you approached God with such lack of formality, He might be offended and not hear your prayers. Where is the balance?

answer

The best examples of talking to God are in the psalms, which are prayers mostly recorded by King David in the Bible. There David shared whatever was in his heart, whether it was fears, concerns, joy, or anger. He simply spoke to God all the time, never losing his reverence for God, but speaking with complete trust and faith, as a child would to a trusted parent. He talked to God.

Those psalms show examples of every emotion common to people. At times, David was afraid for his life, and at other times, he was depressed and wondering if his life had any meaning at all. He wrote his conversations with God when he was furious at someone trying to cause him harm, and he also recorded those conversations when he stood overcome by God's glory and mercy.

While talking to God, David modeled a mature love relationship. He started each prayer conversation out of the emotions of his heart, and always came back to the point of acknowledging God's power, might, and wisdom. He let his conversations with God move him back into the place of trusting God with every aspect of his life, each time asking God to do what He willed. Talking to God is just that—open and honest conversation, but always upholding God in His proper place of reverence.

worth thinking about

▶ **If God created** you and designed the way you are, then He is interested in even the thoughts you have throughout the day.

▶ **You want to hear** every little thing and share whatever is on your mind when you love someone. God loves you, and He wants you to share like that with Him.

▶ **You can talk** to God whenever He crosses your mind throughout the day. A simple, short prayer is enough to feel connected.

> *You did not receive the spirit of bondage again to fear, but you received the Spirit of adoption by whom we cry out, "Abba, Father."*
> Romans 8:15, NKJV

question

Can you pray without knowing the Bible?

The Bible contains God's words, but also encompasses a lot of reading. It can be daunting to sit down and read, knowing that no matter how much you read, plenty remains. You wonder if prayer can be as effective if you have not memorized passages of scripture, or if some of the stories of the Bible are not familiar to you. Knowledge of the Bible certainly helps you to know what things are better to pray for, but it is difficult to know where to start.

answer

God, in His great love, cherishes your prayer. If your prayer is a simple "I love You, God," or a prayer filled with concerns, God hears your every word. Nothing is as beautiful as the prayers of small children, who innocently tell God about their day and their toy that was lost and anything else on their minds. This kind of freedom from worry about how to speak to God makes it much easier to pray. God wants to hear the things that are on your mind and the things that are important to you. He cares about you, not about the way you speak.

It is true that the words in the Bible hold some part of His wondrous being and inscrutable truth. When you read the Bible, you will start to see more of God as you read. You will see His character and learn more about Him. If you read sections of the Bible that address your situation, you will learn to know the will of God and how to pray accordingly. Either way, reading the Bible can help your prayer life.

The bottom line is that the more you know God, the more intimate and powerful your prayers will be. Knowing God comes from time spent with Him in prayer, and time spent reading His Word. The more you pray, the more you will want to pray. Over time, you will grow and mature, both in your relationship with God and in your prayer life. You will be a healthier and happier person, and your prayers will be deeper and richer.

worth thinking about

▶ **The Bible is** very much like God's family album. His history is your history, and you learn about His character by reading the Bible.

▶ **Prayer matures** and grows over time, just as your knowledge of the Bible. Be patient with yourself and take the time to learn.

▶ **Knowing the Bible** lets you pray with more wisdom and assurance, because God provides examples of prayer and His perfect truth for you to use when praying.

> *Understanding your word brings light to the minds of ordinary people.*
> Psalm 119:130, CEV

question

Does God *need* you to pray?

People enjoy being needed. To know that you have what someone else will gratefully receive brings good feelings. When you think about prayer, however, it is difficult to determine if prayer is or is not something God needs. Knowing that prayer pleases God would make it easier to make prayer a habit every day, but understanding just why it pleases God would really answer the question. Does He need you to pray? Or are there other reasons prayer is important to God?

answer

God *wants* you to pray. He *tells* you to. But He does not *need* you to pray. God existed before anything else in the universe. He was God before He ever created people and told them to pray. In the most technical sense, God does not need prayer. He has no need of anything because He is. The concept is difficult to grasp. He did not tell you to pray because He needed something.

God, in His infinite and merciful wisdom, knows that *people* need prayer. Through prayer, people look for and find God's good. Your response and prayer to the God who made you sets in motion a sacred give-and-take that not only works with His purposes on earth, but also allows Him to work in your life. Prayer is one of the grandest and most incredible gifts for communication with God that you can claim. Prayer is your direct line to God. You need to make a deliberate effort to pray.

Without prayer, it is easy to begin to relegate God to a comforting concept or an idea. The living, sustaining hope that stays ignited through your relationship with God will suffer from neglect if you ignore prayer, and the world will seem less controlled by the divine. With the number of vital reasons for prayer in your life, it is a practice and lifestyle you simply cannot neglect.

worth thinking about

▶ **God wants you** to be in touch with Him in prayer and agree with what He is doing. He gives you that privilege freely.

▶ **Prayer is your** sacred duty. God asks you to pray and gives you the means, so to avoid prayer is disobedience to Him.

▶ **No spiritual giants** from throughout history ever gained that position without the practice of prayer. Consider the inspiring stories of Elijah, Daniel, Paul, and countless others.

He who lives a prayerless life lives without God in the world.
Jonathan Edwards

10

Will God do what He wants anyway?

Prayer can seem like a futile exercise if viewed fatalistically. If you believe God always waits to preempt your petitions with His will for every situation, then it will seem that prayer is unnecessary and frustrating. However, in the Bible, God asks people to pray, and to pray always and for every situation. As you pray, agree with God and request His perfect will to come forth and benefit people.

answer

A strange combination of submission to God's authority and contributing to His actions exists in prayer. God is God, and He is perfectly capable of ordering the universe according to His perfect will. And yet He created humans and then gave humans the privilege of interacting with Him in the relationship of prayer. A key to balancing this combination of ideas is to understand the need to acknowledge God as God over all areas of your life. Remembering His authority when you pray helps keep your prayers in balance.

Relationship with God requires acceptance of His rightness over your life. But He asks you to pray, and while you pray, He actually listens to what you have to say. As an example, a story in the Old Testament of the Bible tells of a man named Lot who bargained with God to save his hometown, which teetered on the brink of total destruction because of moral depravity. God listened, and He was willing to give more mercy each time Lot asked, but in the end, God knew what He had to do.

Your responses to God often set in motion either the blessings of God when you act in obedience, or the consequences that come because of sin. He hears prayers and issues the invitation to come and reason with Him Even though there is nothing He has not thought of, it pleases Him when His children pray alongside Him, loving people as He does.

worth thinking about

▶ **At times,** God's plans and purposes remain a mystery, but that mystery needs to propel your faith in prayer and to trust whatever He is doing in your life.

▶ **You can enjoy** releasing the reins to God when you realize doing so means you are free from the worry of what may or may not happen.

▶ **As you grow** in your relationship, you become more convinced that God will never do things that are not in your best interest. It would be against His nature.

> *Trust in the LORD with all your heart, and lean not on your own understanding; in all your ways acknowledge Him, and He shall direct your paths.*
> Proverbs 3:5–6, NKJV

11

Is prayer just to make you feel better about life?

Prayer sometimes sounds like a take-one-every-morning fix for your life. It would make sense that if your life lacked happiness and satisfaction, prayer would be something to try in an effort to be happier. But prayer is not a powerless ritual to be practiced to improve your life. It is a divine connection—a holy God making Himself accessible to mortal human beings in conversation as intimate as friends talking face-to-face.

answer

Prayer does make you feel better about life. But not for the reasons you think. Prayer cannot be checked off a list of things to do every day, like flossing your teeth or walking the dog. Prayer is a living and giving relationship with God. When you meet with God, you experience change.

If you want God's blessing on your life, there is just no alternative to prayer. Prayer is the way you triumph over temptations in your life, the way you ask God to heal the sick and encourage others. Prayer allows you to reach those who do not know God, and help those who have moved away from God. Besides a way to know the will of God, prayer is the only way to accomplish the impossible. Awesome things happen when God's power is released into your life and the lives of others. His power comes because of prayer, and then nothing is the same.

If something changes you and changes the circumstances around you more to the way God wants them to be, you will feel an enjoyable difference in your life. If prayer causes you to feel less fear and anxiety because you trust God more, you will feel a wonderful difference in your life. And if prayer hooks you into the great love of God and enables you to have greater love for others, you will feel a difference in your life. You will be changed.

worth thinking about

- ▶ **Prayer lets you** view the world through different glasses. Seeing things God's way will make your life better.

- ▶ **Joy comes from** your relationship with God, which becomes richer and deeper with time. Happiness comes from the way you look at life. Prayer benefits both.

- ▶ **Prayer brings you** into contact with the living, loving God. That will make you feel better about life.

> Nothing between us and God, our faces shining with the brightness of his face. And so we are transfigured much like the Messiah, our lives gradually becoming brighter and more beautiful as God enters our lives and we become like him.
>
> 2 Corinthians 3:18, THE MESSAGE

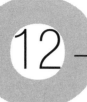

question

If you are happy, why pray?

When life is comfortable and things are going well, you may not feel a need to pray. Often, thoughts of God come more frequently when things are going badly, but you know that you should speak to God at other times as well. The impetus to keep praying even when life is going well springs from a better understanding of the reasons for communicating with God through prayer.

answer

God cares about more than your happiness in life. Even though that happiness seems of utmost importance to you, God wants even more. The Bible says that God's ways are not your ways and that His thoughts are not like your thoughts. Because of that, He puts more importance on your relationship with Him and your obedience to your purpose in life. God sees things through the view of eternity, while you see things as they relate to you today.

God gives you a way to stay in close communication with Him, but He also calls you friend. Imagine the kind of friendship God allows you to share with Him. Not only is He the God of all power and might, but He sent His Son, Jesus, to take away anything that could possibly separate you from Him. He provides you His comfort and gives you healing and freedom. In the words of Jesus, He tells you these things so that His "joy may remain in you, and that your joy may be full" (John 15:11, NKJV).

Prayer is complex and multidimensional and is much more than something you need just when life is hard. Keeping your relationship with God through good times and bad times enables God to be always working in your life, maturing you and changing you for the better. True happiness will come from staying in close connection with God. Let your joy overflow in thanks to God for all the lasting benefits of prayer.

worth thinking about

- ▶ **Fair-weather friends** rarely are true friends. God deserves to be more than a fair-weather friend.

- ▶ **It is better if you** already know God and know His character before you have a need to call on Him when you face trouble. Spend time with Him when things are going well so that you can feel a familiar comfort when times are hard.

- ▶ **If you determine** to pray each time you read the Bible, you have a built-in reminder to pray each time you open it.

> *Every time we reach out and touch Him in prayer, our lives are healed in some way and our faith is increased.*
> Stormie Omartian

13 question

▼

If someone is praying for you, is it enough to help?

You know that God is your source to provide all you need, and He is your help when you are in trouble. When times are tough, you know others are praying for you, but you wonder if that is enough to help you through. It is hard to imagine how much one person's prayers do, or five persons' prayers, but it seems that would be enough to help you. Just how much prayer is enough to help?

answer

▼

Miracles have happened, people have committed their hearts to God, and lives have been saved because someone prayed. There is no question that prayer is more powerful than anyone can ever know. The Bible states that the prayers of a righteous person do much good. It is a blessing to know that someone cares enough for you to pray for your needs.

The prayers of others are valuable, and your confident prayers of trust in God are valuable. Both work to help you have peace of mind when you are going through tough circumstances. Throughout the Bible, you read the phrase "when you pray" and not "if you pray." There is an expectation that you already pray for your own life as well as for others'. This must happen in order to keep the relationship between you and God alive and well. This tells God that you trust Him enough to bring Him your cares.

It is fine to feel gratified and comforted to know that others are praying for you, but you must see to your prayer life as well. Perhaps no one ever reaches a position where prayer is unnecessary. But if prayer truly acts as a catalyst for God's power in your life, brings blessings to you, matures you as a believer, and links you to God's purposes on the earth, then you should always welcome prayer.

worth thinking about

▶ **You can pray** for your own needs, and God will hear. Always pray for your own needs, and then ask for prayer from others.

▶ **If you ask** for prayer from others about a tough situation or need, tell them just enough to pray with understanding.

▶ **Remember to pray** for others so that your focus moves from inward and your own needs to outward and the needs of others.

Don't worry about anything, but pray about everything. With thankful hearts offer up your prayers and requests to God. Then, because you belong to Christ Jesus, God will bless you with peace that no one can completely understand. And this peace will control the way you think and feel.

Philippians 4:6–7, CEV

question

How do you know if God hears your prayer?

Talking to someone face-to-face allows you not only to hear but also to see the person whose response you receive. Being known and heard, along with knowing and hearing the other person, is what makes a good relationship of communication. Prayer, however, can seem to be one-sided and the sound of your own voice like an empty echo. What is it that can assure you God hears your prayers, each and every time you call out to Him?

answer

Knowing the character of God provides the best assurance of prayers heard and answered. Throughout the Bible, God's great love and faithfulness to the people He created shine through. God never fails to hear, or fails to show up, when someone cries out to Him.

The Bible relates story after story of men and women who trusted the love of God as they prayed for their needs, for guidance, for help in trouble, and for comfort. Prayers recorded in the Bible stand as examples of people's trust in God. God's love sings to your heart throughout the Psalms as you read that God hears and lovingly delivers His children out of their troubles.

When Jesus taught His disciples to pray, one of the first things He wanted them to know was that God is sure to hear and answer. He spoke with authority as the Son of God, who knew God's character better than anyone. He told His disciples, "When you pray, go away by yourself, shut the door behind you, and pray to your Father in private. Then your Father, who sees everything, will reward you" (Matthew 6:6, NLT).

God never changes. His promises never fail. Reading about the ways God rewarded those who called on Him builds your trust and faith. He hears your prayers and cares deeply for you.

worth thinking about

▶ Hearts of faith-filled prayer see God and His loving care, while hearts of doubt see only the dark clouds of life.

▶ Reading the Bible pumps up your faith-muscles to believe in the faithfulness of the God you cannot see and in prayer that seems one-sided.

▶ If you want to go to God, you have to first believe that He exists, and then to believe that He cares enough to respond to you.

> *God alone is our salvation. Apart from the Lord, all is lost in darkness. Day and night, our prayers rise to Him, and He hears even the deepest silent cry of our souls. To think of it!—The Almighty one, the powerful Creator of all things, it is He and none other who bends low to listen tenderly to our cries!*
>
> Saint Francis of Assisi

15 question

Do the prayers of one person matter in the world?

When you think of all the believers who pray at any given moment around the world, your prayers may seem to be small. God hears many voices in many languages all at the same time asking for many things. It is hard to imagine how He keeps them all straight, much less how He can pay particular attention to the prayers of just one person. You want to know that your prayers matter.

answer

The same God who spoke of knowing how many hairs are on your head, and who said not even one sparrow falls to the ground without His knowledge, is the God who hears your prayers. God's eyes and ears are on the lookout for each person who loves Him. He sees you, and He hears your prayers. "GOD is always on the alert, constantly on the lookout for people who are totally committed to him" (2 Chronicles 16:9, THE MESSAGE).

God lovingly described how much He valued the prayers of His people when He compared those prayers to golden bowls of incense. That language indicates that God really cherishes your prayers, along with the other prayers reaching His ears. What you bring to Him is of great importance. God is completely powerful and completely amazing, and yet He cherishes the words you speak to Him. If you think about this, you realize that you cannot even fathom the greatness and incredible love of God. No one can.

By remembering and thinking about how much God values your prayers, you can pray believing that anything is possible. Your prayers may change things you could never imagine in places unknown by you. But know that not one word, or one utterance, or even one sigh from you is ever missed by God. When you pray, pray as someone who understands that what you do could have eternal consequences for the good of people around the world.

worth thinking about

▶ The prayers of one person matter to God. He hears every word you utter and every need you give to Him.

▶ God cares for you with intense interest and deep love. Every prayer you speak matters to God because of it. Not even one word escapes His notice.

▶ If you believe that your prayers matter to God, then you will pray with confidence and assurance. What you pray will change, and you will see more of God's power evident in your life.

> *The littlest prayer broadens out by the will of God till it touches all words, conserves all interests, and enhances man's greatest wealth, and God's greatest good.*
>
> E. M. Bounds

How can anyone pray in a stressed-out world?

Never be in a hurry. Do everything quietly and calmly. Don't lose your inner peace for anything whatsoever, even if your whole world seems upset.

Saint Francis de Sales

16 question

Does God care about your opinions on situations?

Caring about each other's opinions is a sign of respect in relationships between two people. You want your thoughts and opinions esteemed by the people you connect with in daily life, and you hope that God also sees your ideas and thoughts as having some value. In order to pray and communicate with God freely and openly, you want to know how He views what you say.

answer

God knows every secret of your heart. No opinion or thought is unknown by Him. He cares about you, and every thought you are thinking. "Be humble in the presence of God's mighty power, and he will honor you when the time comes. God cares for you, so turn all your worries over to him" (1 Peter 5:6–7, CEV).

What precious words from God! He cares about your opinions and knows your thoughts, and if you take those to Him and acknowledge His superior wisdom, He will lift you up. Your circumstances will not press you with feelings of hopelessness and helplessness. You tell God your thoughts, trusting that they are important enough to Him that He will not ignore them or neglect to hear them.

God possesses a rich depth of unsearchable wisdom and knowledge. His ways are beyond understanding and beyond discovery. God knows about all that is happening, and all that will happen, and He best knows how to handle anything you would ever experience in your life. Find the balance that comes from sharing your heart with God, and then ask Him to bring your thinking into line with what He has in mind for you.

worth thinking about

▶ **Some feeling** of insignificance is good in your relationship with God. To acknowledge His greatness is to acknowledge your own need, but with that come humility and the assurance that God cares about your thoughts.

▶ **The only fail-safe** place to express your opinions is with God. He hears, and He reacts to you with love and concern.

▶ **You can trust** that God will move you to a place of believing in His constant good in response to your opinions because you pray.

> *To God, we're not just another face in the crowd. A real relationship is two-sided, and just as we are drawn to know all we can about God, God delights to know everything about us.*
>
> Christa Kinde

17 question

Do prayers for big world issues make a difference?

The problems in the world seem overwhelming. So much poverty, hate, mistreatment of children, and injustice rock the headlines each week that it is hard to think clearly enough to pray. It is also easy to wonder if the prayers you speak to God about these matters can actually have an effect on issues this deep and entrenched in the ways of the world. Keeping an understanding of what God says about prayer can make all the difference when praying about serious issues.

answer

God cares deeply about the problems in the world. When you have a relationship with Him, God allows you to feel particularly concerned about these issues, too. The Bible says that your prayers are important. "The earnest prayer of a righteous person has great power and produces wonderful results" (James 5:16, NLT). Even if your prayers seem small in the face of huge problems in the world, you still make a difference. You may be part of God's plan as you bring your concern to Him. Your compassion may lead you to be part of the solution for people who are suffering, and by showing compassion, you represent God to those caught up in difficulties.

When you see sin and evil trying to get the upper hand in the world, you must not despair. God has authority over the world, and His kingdom is love and justice. When you pray in faith, you agree that He is God over all, and you welcome His action for others. Never lose heart, for you can reach far-flung places with your prayers. You can bolster missionaries and encourage those who suffer persecution for God's sake. There is much power and influence in your prayers, as you keep to God's plan and purposes for the world.

worth thinking about

▶ **God's love extends** to all people in the world. Praying brings His character into your life, so His cares become your cares.

▶ **Learning the will** of God by reading the Bible also teaches you to pray His way, and that ensures your prayers have an effect, even on issues affecting many people.

▶ **Knowing what** the Bible says about the power of God also lets you know what you become part of by praying.

> *Let us pray diligently. Prayer is a mighty weapon if used with earnestness and sincerity, without drawing attention to ourselves. It has turned back wars, and benefited an entire undeserving nation.*
>
> Saint John Chrysostom

question

▼

What if others are praying about an issue in a different way than you?

As you gather with other believers and pray together, you may become aware that some are praying about an issue in a different way than you. You may wonder if you are praying correctly or if they are, and it causes you to doubt your words to God. Since differences will always exist, how do you handle knowing that there are various prayers going to God about the same issue?

answer

▼

There are at least two sides to every situation. If you said the word *blue* to a roomful of people, some would think of the color of blue like the sky, some would think of being blue and sad, and still others would think the word meant what the wind did as it moved. Much of life is a beautiful mystery, but Scripture also states that God revealed some of His mystery to you through His Spirit. If you know God and listen to His voice and what He is sharing with you, you know what He is telling you to pray. God may ask you to pray for one aspect of a situation, and prompt someone else to pray about another aspect.

Concerns about your prayer life belong to you and God, and the prayer lives of others belong to God as well. You cannot judge what another has heard from God about what to pray, just as someone else cannot judge what you have heard from God.

God is sovereign and all-knowing, and He will not be blown off course even if someone is praying about a situation in a totally opposite direction from you. God will work His will and purposes, and you alone are responsible for what you think and pray. Always ask God to search your heart to see if there are any sinful motives behind what you pray and do. By keeping yourself honest and open before God, you will be sure that you are praying what He wants.

worth thinking about

▶ **When you do** not know what to pray, pray the prayer that is always right: "God, may Your will be done."

▶ **Pray with confidence** and be faithful to what God shares with you. Refrain from adding what sounds good from someone else's prayer to your own, unless God leads you to do so.

▶ **If you come** under criticism for the way you pray, take that criticism to God in prayer. He will show you if you need to change the way you pray.

> *Prayer is coming into perfect fellowship and oneness with God. If the Son of God has been formed in us through regeneration (see Galatians 4:19), then He will continue to press on beyond our common sense and will change our attitude about the things for which we pray.*
> Oswald Chambers

19

question

Does prayer change the future?

When you believe in God, you believe that God knows what the future holds for each person. Therefore, when you think about prayer as a powerful line of communication to God about people and circumstances, you may wonder whether the things you pray for can change what will happen in the future, and whether things should be changed. You want to pray in the way that God wants, and in the way that leaves decisions regarding the future to Him.

answer

The future rests in God's hands. In His immensely complex understanding, God knows what the best is for each life, and what is needed for each person and in each situation. And yet God allows His people to help fulfill His purposes. Think of it this way: as you pray, you become a worker alongside God helping to bring about His will. Prayer is more than you can imagine and cannot be taken lightly.

A co-laborer will help accomplish something intentionally with another. It is an incredible blessing to be considered part of God's work in the world, and it is something to be taken quite seriously. God said that all things work together for good when you love Him, so in some sense, this great will and purpose of God's can happen if and when His children pray and join Him in His work. That condition is by God's choice, not because God has any limitations.

God does have a good purpose for those who believe on His name. Prayer and the intimacy of your relationship with Him work together to bring you into agreement with God's purposes for your life and the lives of others. It brings you to love Him and welcome His best and greatest purposes for your life. Your love relationship with Him blooms and ushers in greater good and greater blessing as you pray more and more in alignment with His will.

worth thinking about

▶ **Followers of God** have no reason to fear the future. God assures you that He will make all things work for good in your life if you follow Him.

▶ **The need to know** the future by some means usually reflects fear about the future. Resting in faith in God eliminates the need to know the future.

▶ **If you do not know** how to pray about the future you face, pray that God's will be done. That is actually a prayer that reflects great faith and trust.

> *Prayer does not change God's mind; it changes ours.*
> Author Unknown

20 question

How do you learn to pray?

Not everyone has a mentor or a special person in life to teach and instruct them in spiritual matters. The Bible says to pray, and even to pray without ceasing, but it is hard to grasp just what prayer is and how to pray from the pages of the Bible. Because the disciples were people who also needed instruction in prayer, the chapters in the Bible that record Jesus' teaching to them can also give you powerful lessons in prayer today.

answer

The disciples asked Jesus to teach them to pray. Jesus modeled prayer as no one else could. He was in a vital, living relationship with the Father, and He relied on Him for everything He needed. He rose early in the morning to spend time with God before anything else. He did nothing without asking God first. Seeing this vibrant and passionate example of a lifestyle of prayer, the disciples asked about it. Jesus responded with a model of prayer.

The Lord's Prayer is the model Jesus gave the disciples to teach them the important elements of prayer. It is a step-by-step diagram for putting together prayer that honors and pleases God while at the same time addressing human needs. This is an excellent place to start exploring what prayer is and how to keep first things first. It starts with honoring God and ends with requests for the needs of the day.

Other prayers by men and women of God are recorded in the pages of the Bible. Each one captures important aspects of those people's relationships with God, and each one is a valuable aid as you learn to pray. God honored the prayers you see written, and circumstances changed because of the prayers. If you do have a spiritual mentor in your life, ask that person how he prays. The experience of others can encourage you in the same way as the prayers recorded in the Bible.

worth thinking about

▶ **Reading the prayers** of others, particularly pillars of faith past and present, can enlighten your prayer life. Their spiritual maturity helps develop yours.

▶ **A key to effective** prayer is developing a focus outward at least as much as your focus inward on things that concern you.

▶ **If you never pray** with others, you will never experience the rich and varied expressions of prayer in the lives of others. These prayers may inspire you.

> *Prayer is often expressed in words, but it is not the words that God recognizes as prayer. It is not the cry of the lips, but the cry of the heart that God hears. We are living prayers.*
>
> Jennifer Kennedy Dean

question

Is there a format to use in prayer?

When you begin praying, you want to know if there is a right way to pray. Without an instruction manual, it is hard to know how to structure your prayers, and it's hard to know if there are certain parts that make up an acceptable prayer. Using a structure for your prayers would make it easier to get started and would seem a better way to pray than to just blurt out what you need.

answer

A model or structure of prayer can help you remember to be thorough in prayer. A prayer structure can also give you another way to pray to change your routine. The simplest and most common model of prayer focuses first on God and His greatness, and then on the needs you bring to God. You will find that as you worship God first, your faith is higher and your own needs will seem smaller. This is a good way to start.

Some people employ another structure as they learn to pray freely. Each letter of the acronym ACTS stands for a section of prayer. The letter *A* stands for *adoration*, starting your prayer with praise for the God who is above all things. The letter *C* reminds you to *confess* your sins and ask for God's loving forgiveness, so your heart is pure. The letter *T* is for *thanksgiving*, prompting you to praise God for His blessings and goodness in your life. And finally, the *S* stands for *supplication*, or asking God for the needs you have in your life.

Models teach ways to organize your prayers that are God-pleasing and help you keep the right focus in your words. Like training wheels, when you are ready to move away from prayer models, you can push off and soar with prayers that come freely from your heart.

worth thinking about

▶ **Starting your prayer** journey with a little help from a popular format is no different from learning any new skill. You may learn much faster with a little help.

▶ **If a prayer format** becomes a crutch to use all the time, the vitality of your prayers will diminish. You need to develop your relationship with God.

▶ **Balance is always** important in everything you do and applies even to prayer. Remembering God's greatness first keeps everything that comes after in greater balance.

> *Jesus in effect taught us through this sample prayer how to pray, what our attitude should be in prayer, how we should approach God, and what we should talk to God about.*
>
> Rick Osbourne

question

Is formal language necessary when praying?

Formal language with great words and fancy phrases sounds impressive and even beautiful. For many, this language pattern of prayer formed the structure of the worship services of their youth. While it may be tempting to believe God enjoys that kind of sophisticated prayer, God listens to much more than the words you speak. He searches your heart and knows what you think and feel. Any prayer to Him need not be as formal as you think.

answer

You might come from a church tradition where formal language is the most comfortable to you, but God does not require fancy language. Because He created people and the language of communication used by each people group, He knows that crafting words in complex ways speaks deeply of emotion and ideas. Any piece of classic literature reflects the beauty of language and thought developed over the centuries.

His complete understanding of your thoughts, emotions, and beliefs is just one of the marvelous mysteries of God. Because He has such loving knowledge of you, you need not carefully craft your words to convince Him of your sincerity or need. He already knows what you need and how deeply you love Him, and His pleasure comes when you trust Him enough to talk to Him.

The Bible says that God does not see as humans see, as in the tendency to judge by outward appearances. God looks at the heart of a person, and there finds the truest expression of relationship and communication. Prayer is an expression of confident trust in God. God's response does not change based on the value of your words. Your style of prayer doesn't need to be formal. It simply must flow from what matters to you.

worth thinking about

▶ **God created language** for the communication of people. He chose not to make language complicated for everyday use, so prayer can be the same.

▶ **God is the One** who hears your prayers. Because He knows what is in your heart, He also knows the way you communicate.

▶ **Thoughts from your heart** just may be too deep for words, no matter how eloquent. Let them find expression in your words as they may.

> *God doesn't demand that we pray in King James English, or even with eloquence. Every feeble, stumbling prayer uttered by a believer is heard by God. A cry, a sigh, a "Help!" are all prayers, according to the Psalms.*
> Billy Graham

question

Whom do you pray to—God, Jesus, or the Holy Spirit?

God is the Father, the Son, and the Holy Spirit—all in one being, sometimes referred to as the Trinity. The Bible refers to each one, and it seems they all overlap in its pages. When talking to a person on the telephone, it helps to know the identity of the person you are addressing. That enables you to decide how to speak to him. It is the same with prayer. You need to know to whom you are speaking, and how to communicate in the most effective way.

answer

God created prayer. He began loving dialogue with Adam and Eve in the Garden of Eden. As the One who created them, God wanted Adam and Eve to share their hearts and needs with Him. That close communication of love continues when prayers lift to God in faith and trust. The One who made you knows your needs before you even pray.

Jesus taught His disciples to pray to God, reminding them of His authority when He said that He would do whatever they asked in Jesus' name. Jesus wanted God to be honored by people who would trust and pray to Him. Because of the love of God, Jesus Himself prays for *you*. In Hebrews

7:25, the Bible describes Jesus as "able to save to the uttermost those who come to God through Him, since He always lives to make intercession for them" (NKJV).

Before Jesus left earth to go back to the Father, He consoled His followers by saying He would not leave them alone, but with a Comforter, the Holy Spirit. E. M. Bounds described Jesus' gift this way: "He (the Holy Spirit) works mightily in us so that we can pray mightily. He enables us to pray always and ever according to the will of God."

Your prayers are precise conversations because you pray to God, who knows you more completely than anyone else; you pray in Jesus' name, who *Himself* prays for you from heaven; and you pray with the Holy Spirit, who helps you know how to pray.

worth thinking about

▶ The Bible records God's invitation to prayer again and again: "Call on Me."

▶ If Jesus intercedes for you, and the Holy Spirit guides your prayers, you can be confident that God knows your needs.

▶ When words are not enough, the Holy Spirit helps you with prayers that come straight from the heart of God.

How blessed we are to be in relationship with our God, who gives us all we need for a life of prayer.
Cynthia Heald

question
▼

Is it all right to sometimes pray in different ways?

Praying the same way every day can sometimes become difficult. For some, sitting in a chair may create feelings of anxiousness. Others find they cannot kneel in the very traditional way of praying. Some may find that after a time of praying silently, they can hardly keep words from springing from their mouths—loudly. And sometimes, even speaking to God may seem tedious if done the same way every day as though from a script.

answer
▼

People have prayed to God in many ways. Some phrases in the Psalms concerning prayer describe such things as crying out with a loud voice, declaring with strong words, meditating on your bed, praying with a troubled soul, praising the Lord, and singing to the Lord. People have always prayed while moving, dancing, grieving, singing, or even while being silent. Examples in the Bible show this clearly. Some prayed out in the middle of the desert while others prayed on a rooftop, but all prayed.

God created the universe, so He is the embodiment of variety and wonder. He created people in His own image, so He knows that each person captures part of the creativity and wonder that are His.

There is no right or wrong way to pray. If you find you need to change your position, or if you need to pray while walking or to yell your prayers, then do so if it honors God and brings you closer to Him. Sing, shout, whisper, or cry. God knows your every emotion and thought, and you need to reach Him in a way that is meaningful and functional for you. When you find the ways that work best for you, you may even find your prayers become more intense as you lose the distraction of a method that does not reflect you as a person.

worth thinking about

▶ **The measure** of a style of prayer is whether it honors God and facilitates your petitions. If it detracts from your communication with God, then avoid it.

▶ **Some people** find that certain habits enhance the depth of their prayers. Some people walk in prayer gardens, make the sign of the cross on their bodies, or pray in a special place.

▶ **Prayer must be** as individual as the person who is praying. You can be true to yourself even when talking to God.

> *Prayer is a way of relating to God, not a skill set like double-entry bookkeeping. . . . It should hardly surprise God that we respond in a way that reflects our true self.*
>
> Philip Yancey

question

How do you know whom to pray for?

When you begin to pray, your heart enlarges to encompass more and more people. You become more sensitive to the needs of those around you because you are praying, and you develop more compassion as your times with God influence your thoughts and concerns. The hard thing is to be able to know for whom to pray and for what needs. Remembering important needs becomes difficult in light of busy schedules and hectic lifestyles.

answer

As you pray, you become more and more convinced of the benefits of prayer. You see the blessings in your own life, and you see the blessings in the lives of the ones you ask God to help. You want to pray for as many people as need it, but it is hard to know who needs prayer the most.

God knows which people need prayer and which ones have others praying for them. You have no way to determine by yourself which person needs prayer the most. There is no hard-and-fast rule, but if your heart moves with compassion for someone in need, then you need to pray. It could be someone you pass on the street, or it could be your neighbor or a friend. Feelings of compassion form a call for help from God's hotline.

At other times, your list may be too long to cover each time you pray, even if you list the names and keep them where you pray. In order to pray according to God's will, ask Him to show you which people need prayer that day. You will get a feeling of direction, or certain names will come to your mind, and you can pray the way God wants. If you leave the selection or decision to Him, you know that you are not making a mistake when you pray.

worth thinking about

▶ A Yiddish proverb states that if you pray for another, you yourself will be helped. Prayer never benefits in one direction only, but blesses the person who prays as well as the person who is prayed for.

▶ You do not need to pray for each person you know every single day. If God moves your heart to particular people, then pray for them.

▶ Sometimes prayer requires action. You may feel prompted to help the person for whom you pray and meet some physical needs as well.

> *At this end of day I want to gather up all the people I care about and ask for help for them. Those who are in trouble, those who need healing. I'm so busy and the list is long . . . if I don't keep this standing appointment with God, I might not do it.*
> Marjorie Holmes

Is prayer really as difficult as it seems?

Do let us believe that God's call
to much prayer need not be a
burden and cause of continual
self-condemnation. He means
it to be a joy! He can make it
an inspiration, giving us
strength for all our work.

Andrew Murray

question

▼

Do you have to pray in the morning?

For some, mornings race by, hectic and full of chaos. Children off to school, parents off to work. The atmosphere is not exactly conducive to prayer. The Bible doesn't set certain times of the day to pray, so you wonder if it is necessary to find a way to fit prayer into an already overloaded time slot in the early hours of the day. It seems that one more thing might unbalance your day.

answer

▼

Many people in the Bible made a point of meeting with God in the morning. David, as he wrote in the Psalms, greeted God and poured out his heart. His words convey a special delight in those times of intimacy with God. Mark 1:35 states that Jesus woke and left the house while it was still dark to pray in a quiet place. He knew that communicating with the Father before the day began would give Him the strength and wisdom He needed to touch many lives and to teach others.

Nothing in the Bible indicates that prayer must take place in the morning. Prayer any time of the day or night builds your faith and connects you with God. Prayer throughout the day lets you walk in greater faith to meet any challenge or difficulty. You gain more grace and peace as you pray any time of day. Of course, the main idea is to pray, and to pray as often as you can.

An old saying states that a day hemmed in prayer is less likely to unravel. Benefits of prayer in the morning are indisputable, but when to pray remains the decision of the individual. The best time for you to pray is whatever time works best for you to be able to lift your concerns and needs to God.

worth thinking about

- ▶ **Prayer in the morning** says, "Good morning, God! What do You have planned today?" and prayer in the evening says, "Thanks, God, for a great day!"

- ▶ **Starting the day** by asking for God's protection and direction covers anything that might happen. You can walk in greater peace, knowing that nothing that comes that day comes by accident.

- ▶ **By addressing God** in the first part of the day, you will find it easier to keep Him in your mind throughout the day. This is what starts the practice of unceasing prayer.

> *The morning prayer determines the day. Squandered time of which we are ashamed, temptations to which we succumb, weaknesses and lack of courage in work, disorganization and lack of discipline in our thoughts and in our conversation with other men, all have their origin most often in the neglect of morning prayer.*
>
> Dietrich Bonhoeffer

question

How often should you pray?

Once you start your prayer journey, you find that the Bible does not specifically dictate the number of times you should pray each day. It is easy to fall into thinking that if some praying is good, then much praying many times a day is better. You can also get discouraged if you feel you are missing the mark in frequency of prayer, and you might feel like giving up. Neither view represents the right idea about prayer. Prayer is not a thing to do; prayer is a relationship to cherish and grow.

answer

Many psalms in the Bible talk about praying in the morning. Jesus rose early and met with God in the mornings before spending time with anyone. Just as many psalms mention David's praying on his bed at night. In the New Testament, you read an admonition to pray without ceasing. These examples encourage prayer at any time of the day or night, but they do not demand a certain number of times to prove devotion to God. You need to find the times that work best for you and to schedule prayer as you would schedule anything else important.

The truth is, the more you want God in your life, the more you should pray. Your relationship will grow with the time you invest in it. Because prayer is living communication with God, your relationship can only get better as you spend more time in it. You will begin to know more and more about God's character and truths as you spend more time concentrating on Him.

Prayer is a wonderful avenue for going right to the source and for availing yourself of God's strength. You can go to God at any time with any problem. You can share your joy, ask for help, confide in God. Prayer enables the believer to access God at any time, and to become all that God intends. By giving God time out of your day, you let Him know He is important to you, and that you want to draw close to Him.

worth thinking about

▶ **Leonard Ravenhill** has said that no man is greater than his prayer life. Prayer unlocks your life to allow God's healing and transforming power to change you for the better.

▶ **Mother Teresa** succinctly said, "The more you pray, the easier it becomes. The easier it becomes, the more you will pray." This is truly a win-win situation.

▶ **The more prayer,** the more power of God evidenced in your life. That provides a compelling incentive to pray more frequently.

> *Prayer is the most important thing in my life.*
> *If I should neglect prayer for a single day,*
> *I should lose a great deal of the fire of faith.*
> Martin Luther

28

Can you just tell God how you feel?

Sometimes the feelings you have of anger, embarrassment, or jealousy seem too unseemly to bring to God, who is holy. Human emotions and thoughts become messy and complicated. You may hesitate to bring those emotions to God in prayer, but your life remains affected by those feelings. How can you approach God in a respectful way and find relief from the things that affect you so strongly?

answer

David poured out his heart to God in the Psalms—his anger, resentment, fear, and tears. Moses told God of his fear of speaking to people. Jonah went so far as to tell God he did not want to speak to the people who needed to hear from God. Jesus, before He was crucified, told God He wished He did not have to go through what lay before Him. He honestly told God what He felt, but He still committed His obedience to God's plan.

David, Moses, Jonah, even Jesus—they all shared their honest feelings with God, who knew all their feelings anyway. Instead of just complaining, each one of them eventually came to a place of acknowledging God and His greatness and goodness, and moved on. In Psalm 38:9

David said, "All my desire is before You; and my sighing is not hidden from You" (NKJV). He went on to ask God for His help with the troubles he feared.

The chief motivation of pouring out your feelings to God should always be that of honesty before God, but it should also be a sincere desire for God's healing and transformation. God knows every nuance and thought in your heart, but He wants to be trusted enough to be told and to be asked for help. Nothing in honest prayer to God will offend Him or stand between God and you. Keep your heart looking for God's highest purposes and grace in your life.

worth thinking about

▶ Bringing your feelings to God with the expectation of His transformation is the kind of prayer John Calvin described as the chief exercise of faith, by which you daily receive God's benefits.

▶ Honesty before God brings humility, which pleases Him. A humble person submits to God's authority and to His perfect will.

▶ Some people stay stuck in a place ruled by emotion. Unless transformation follows, emotion can stunt your spiritual growth.

> Our Lord invites us to come to him as we are, pretending about nothing, feeling our pain, admitting our rage, and longing to satisfy our souls with rich food.
>
> Larry Crabb

question

Do you have to pray aloud?

The fear of praying aloud affects many people. Fear of speaking in public ranks number one for most adults. That fear certainly makes it difficult to think about praying in front of other people, and maybe it affects whether you pray aloud in your own time with God. Many occasions arise in fellowship with other believers, and you need to know whether you can choose to pray that way without displeasing God.

answer

God can certainly hear you when you pray silently since He knows your very thoughts. In the Old Testament, Jesus discouraged overly loud, bragging prayers. He told people to pray to their Father in secret. There is a time and place for praying aloud. His words were meant to challenge those who prayed for reasons other than relationship with God.

Just as no two people have the same personalities and abilities, each person has one or more styles of prayer that work best. Some people use words easily and enjoy leading prayer or speaking in front of groups. They can think on their feet and do not get flustered. Others find quiet prayer most effective, and they need not try to force a different style to fit in. God hears all types of prayer, calm and impassioned, and does not judge the need by the volume accomplished.

Prayer is a continuing relationship, and all healthy relationships grow and change over time. You may not be comfortable praying aloud in a group of people now, but that may also change in the future. The important thing is to keep open the line of communication between you and God at all times.

worth thinking about

▶ **Communication with God** flows from a heart as simple as a child's, without self-consciousness or insecurity. Just pray your feelings of joy, sorrow, or need for assurance to Him.

▶ **If you can pray** aloud in a group, you can help others find the direction and answers they seek. You may be an encouragement or inspiration for someone else.

▶ **No one can judge** your relationship with God by whether you pray in front of others. Only God sees your heart and knows your thoughts.

Prayer turns the eye and the heart heavenward with a child's longings, a child's trust, and a child's expectancy. To hallow God's name, to speak it with bated breath, to hold it sacredly— this also belongs to prayer.

E. M. Bounds

30

question

Why is it important to include praise to God?

The word *praise* comes up in the Bible frequently both as a command and as an expression of the goodness of God. The greater part of the Book of Psalms includes praise. The New Testament admonishes you to praise God at all times, but knowing the importance of praise makes including it in your prayers much easier. You know that God knows how great He is, but it is not clear why you need to remind Him each time you pray.

answer

The sheer magnificence of God boggles the mind. He is and always has been. He will always be. Never has a time been when God was not present. His holiness demands recognition and praise. Praise acknowledges that you know who God is and that you hold His awesome being in highest regard. Praise at the beginning of prayer focuses your mind and helps keep the magnitude of God always in front of you.

The Book of Luke states that praise is so important, "the stones would immediately cry out" if those who praised were silent (19:40, NKJV). God has a strong and compelling reason for you to praise Him, and He will even prompt inanimate rocks to give Him the praise and worship He deserves. God's greatness is more than the human mind can comprehend, and even that thought alone can bring you to expressions of praise.

Unlike a dictator who orders praise, God asks for praise. To keep your relationship in proper balance, He asks of you only what should come naturally in light of the unmerited grace God exhibits, the love He pours out, the needs He fills, and the lives He graciously changes. God is worthy of all praise. Start your prayer with praise and see how all other things fall into place after acknowledgment of His greatness.

worth thinking about

▶ **Praise of God** can only deepen your relationship with Him as you focus on all He is for you, and all that He does for you.

▶ **Praise changes** a dark outlook on life into one that is bathed in the light of the hope that comes only from the one true God.

▶ **Lips that praise** God please Him, so you can know that He smiles on you as you start your prayer with praise.

> *When we worship Him, we have a renewed sense of His presence. Praising God glorifies Him and invites His presence to invade our lives and circumstances in a powerful way. When you are in His presence, things do not remain the same.*
> Stormie Omartian

question

Is thankfulness an important part of prayer?

Being thankful is easier some days than others. When your list of needs and concerns is long, it seems prudent to get right to asking for what you need. Stopping to thank God is good, but hard to remember. You know that as you interact with others, it means much to be thanked for what you do. People who never thank others often get less help as time goes on. You do not want a lack of gratitude to interfere with your interaction with God.

answer

The Bible states that in all things and at all times you should give thanks to God. Because God knows all things, you know He is aware of your gratitude for all He's done, but there are no exceptions in telling you to thank God.

In the Book of Luke, Jesus met ten people afflicted with the disease of leprosy on the road as He traveled. They asked for healing from their misery, so Jesus told them to go and show themselves to the priests to affirm their healing. The account said that only one of the people blessed by the touch of Jesus returned to thank Him.

Jesus told the man to rise and go, for his faith had made him well.

The pause to stop and thank Jesus correlated with faith and the fullness of healing for the man that day. Giving thanks shows you understand fully that divine events come only from the hand of God. When you thank God for the provision for each day, you tell Him you appreciate His loving care for you, and at the same time you acknowledge His perfect will and rule over your life. Your relationship with Him grows, and His peace guards your heart as you gratefully focus on Him.

worth thinking about

▶ **You are to ask** for whatever you need with thanksgiving in your heart. This shows your trust that God, who never fails, will fill your need.

▶ **When your heart** is humble enough to thank God, it is also fertile ground for God's transformation and change. Thanksgiving opens your heart to His best for you.

▶ **Thanking God** for a simple meal reminds you that every bite you take, every breath you breathe, and everything you enjoy all come from His hand.

> *God is always good to us, always faithful to us, always working so diligently in our lives. He is always doing something for us and acting in our best interest, so we need to respond by letting Him know we appreciate everything.*
>
> Joyce Meyer

32
question
What does it mean to pray a blessing on someone?

The term *blessing* seems rarely used in today's society. The dictionary definition describes any utterance of good wishes or things that contribute to happiness or well-being. God's definition of blessing in prayer contains what is good, but also adds the dimension of His special favor and purpose. When you think about blessing, it can seem like something that is strictly God's responsibility, so it is amazing to know that He asks believers to bless others.

answer

God blesses you by the grace, mercy, and love He extends into your life. Without those blessings, your life would be more difficult and static. The changes that mature you in your spiritual life come through the blessing of God. He uses His expression of blessing to transform you into His image and to equip you to live life with His strength and power rather than to live in your own strength.

Jesus taught His disciples the character and beliefs God would particularly bless, which included meekness, mercy, peacemaking, and spiritual hunger. Developing the traits that please Him makes you a blessing and someone who walks in the blessing of God.

In Old Testament times, there was a priestly blessing ordered given to the Israelites. The words from the Book of Numbers are familiar to many: "The LORD bless you and keep you; the LORD make His face shine upon you, and be gracious to you; the LORD lift up His countenance upon you, and give you peace" (6:24–26, NKJV). Speaking words of blessing in prayer over another person asks God's favor and goodness on him, and both God's words from the Bible and words of your own bring about blessing.

worth thinking about

▶ God says to bless those who persecute you. This counterintuitive reaction to people who hurt or oppress you opens them to God's power and love.

▶ Blessing flows from love. The more love in your life, the more you will bless others by your prayers and by your actions.

▶ Many people have never experienced blessings prayed over them. Their lives can be enriched if you bless them in the name of the Lord.

> *Let me tell you a guaranteed by-product of sincerely seeking His blessing: Your life will become marked by miracles. . . . God's power to accomplish great things suddenly finds no obstruction in you. You're moving His direction. You're praying for exactly what God desires. Suddenly the unhindered forces of heaven can begin to accomplish God's perfect will—through you.*
> Bruce Wilkinson

question

How do you tell God what you and others need?

Telling someone what you need may be uncomfortable and make you feel that you are complaining. But God tells you that He wants you to bring everything that troubles you or that you need to His attention. He wants to hear things that are big, and He wants to hear things that are small if they are important to you. You must find a way to pray for yourself, and to intercede and pray for others, that is comfortable enough that you can do it whenever needed.

answer

The best way to share with God your needs and others' needs is to picture the way you would share with a loving and trusted parent. You can ask God with confidence when you bring those requests, because the Bible gives multitudes of prayer examples for every type of need. God cares for you, and He cares for anything of concern to you.

God welcomes your requests and eagerly awaits each one. He does not miss one word. The love He feels for you and the willingness He has for answering your prayers should make you less self-conscious about asking for things. When you read the Bible, you get a strong sense of what God sees as important, and you start placing importance on the same things. Your prayers constantly change and evolve as you become more and more mature.

Along with the freedom you have to ask God, you need to go to Him with the expectation that God answers prayer both for you and for others. When you ask Him confidently and steadily, and then leave the requests in His care, you will have greater peace. The peace will grow, and your prayers will become more trust-filled. You will find joy in praying for others.

worth thinking about

▶ When you pray for other people, you become part of God's work in their lives.

▶ When you pray for other people, you demonstrate and express God's love for them.

▶ Caring for others through a willingness to pray for them keeps your focus from turning inward and stunting your spiritual growth. Praying for others expands your heart and increases your love.

> *The prayer of intercession is the . . . level of prayer which we share the burden of Christ for a person, circumstances, or need anywhere in the world.*
> Paul Y. Cho

question

How do you pray the words of the Bible?

When you pray, you want to use the most effective language to convey your needs and concerns to God. Sometimes it is a struggle to know what you should pray for yourself or for others. The Bible is a resource. It is the written Word of God. It contains love letters from God to you. If you pray, you must make use of the best tool and most encouraging words you will ever read.

answer

Probably the strongest example of praying, or using the words of the Bible, is that of Jesus, when He was fasting in the desert for a long period of time. Satan went to Him and tempted Him to change stones into bread to fill His stomach. He tempted Him to prove His power and to worship the enemy. With each temptation, Jesus answered with a strong "It is written . . ." Once He spoke the words from the Bible, the devil had no grounds to torment Him.

Certainly, there is an answer in the Bible to every temptation or struggle. To pray God's words, you can read aloud the scriptures that God has put on your mind.

Place your name in each verse as a promise to you. When tempted, you can speak aloud the scripture that gives you the most strength as a reminder to the enemy that you are not standing alone.

If God causes a Bible verse to stand out strongly to you for your situation, personalize the verse and pray it. The Bible is powerful, and every chapter contains wisdom that can change your life. Use the inspiration of the Bible to help you when you pray. Use examples from the Bible to help you know what to ask of God when you are praying. God gave the written Bible as a lifeline to His people.

worth thinking about

► **Isaiah 62:6 says** to remind God of the promises He's made to you. The reminder is for your benefit, not for God's. It builds your faith.

► **The words** in the Bible have life, and when you use them to pray, you bring that life into the situation or person.

► **You become more** like God as you pray the words He gave you. Spending time in the Bible changes the way you think and pray.

> *In praying Scripture, I not only find myself in intimate communication with God, but my mind is being retrained, or renewed (Romans 12:2), to think His thoughts about my situation rather than mine.*
>
> Beth Moore

35

What is the Lord's Prayer?

When Jesus lived with His disciples, they learned from Him each day. He taught them by modeling the ideal of spiritual life and faith, and much of what He modeled was His prayer life and constant devotion to the Father. To help them understand, He taught with clear illustrations and examples, as well as with parables. The model prayer was later named the Lord's Prayer, and it illustrated perfect prayer.

answer

Because Jesus' disciples asked Him how to pray, He gave them a model that addressed all the needs the people could have in a way that pleased God. The first part focused on God, and placed Him first, where He should be in your priorities. When Jesus prayed, "Our Father in heaven, hallowed be Your name," He taught them to recognize the holy and perfect God, who is powerful and who also allows people to be close enough to call Him their Father.

The next section acknowledged that God is sovereign and has authority over everything. Jesus taught them to pray that the kingdom of God would come and that His will would be done, which proclaims His rightful position over the entire world. By proclaiming that, the disciples were standing in agreement that God reigned over their lives, and the lives of those around them. They also longed to see His perfect will in operation on earth in their lifetimes.

The model prayer addressed the needs of the disciples and addresses the needs of believers today as well. Jesus taught the disciples to ask God to provide whatever they would need that day, and to ask not only for forgiveness for their sins, but also for the ability to forgive others. And last, the model prayer Jesus gave His disciples illustrated the need to pray for protection from temptation and for deliverance from the enemy.

worth thinking about

▶ Jesus taught by modeling not only the way to pray, but also the habit and lifestyle of prayer. The Lord's Prayer was just part of what He taught.

▶ Reciting this prayer merits no special blessing; instead, it allows you to pray in a balanced way that pleases God.

▶ Every method or form of prayer helps you pray until you feel comfortable, and then your prayers will grow and change with your spiritual growth.

Although it's a great prayer to memorize and use in its original form, what Jesus was teaching his disciples went far beyond repeating the specific words.

Rick Osbourne

question

▼

Is it enough to say only the Lord's Prayer daily?

Because the Lord's Prayer addresses every aspect of prayer that pleases God, it seems that it would be sufficient simply to pray only that prayer each day. While that may be true, the danger of communicating with God through the same prayer every day is that praying is then apt to become just a routine, without the care that a good relationship demands. Praying the prayer Jesus taught can be a meaningful practice, but only if you take care to keep it fresh.

answer

▼

Before Jesus taught the disciples to pray this way, He warned them about the danger of praying meaningless words and long phrases meant only to impress. He said those prayers would not be heard. That is a stern warning and something you do not want to experience. Prayer goes to God, and cannot be used as a way to boast some spiritual status.

On the other hand, many churches use standard prayers as a part of the worship service. Those words are prayed each week and can be spiritually edifying. As a form of worship, they bring the congregation into unity by praying the same words to God.

Only God judges the hearts of people, and He knows when prayers are from the heart. Ask yourself if you understand what the prayer is saying. With care and thoughtfulness, repeated prayers can enhance your relationship with God. If you take the time to grasp each phrase, or even to pause between each phrase to wait for any other promptings from God, you can deepen the meaning of the prayer. Many times, however, praying what is on the heart will be the way that most effectively allows you to speak with God and to continue building your relationship.

worth thinking about

▶ There are no shortcuts to prayer if you want a relationship with God. Relationships take time.

▶ Use the model prayer as a springboard to deeper and more heartfelt prayer. Your prayers will grow over time.

▶ Pray with understanding, and pray what God brings to your mind as well. He will lead you into greater intimacy with Him if you allow.

When you pray, don't babble on and on as people of other religions do. They think their prayers are answered merely by repeating their words again and again.
Matthew 6:7, NLT

question

Can you write down your prayers to God?

Some people learn by seeing and remembering; others need to take notes or make lists in order to remember. Learning styles differ from person to person, as does the way a person relates to the surrounding environment. Certain cues cause certain people to engage thoroughly with conversation, while the same cues might do nothing for another person. Prayer is a method of relating to someone else, and so it makes sense that prayer can be just as individual as each person who prays.

answer

The Bible contains many written prayers. The Book of Psalms was written primarily by King David hundreds of years ago, and it still inspires with its honesty and emotion. Throughout the written history and stories of the Bible, certain prayers recorded illustrate devoted people calling on God's name for His mercy, His protection, and His goodness. God talked about written words when He said that His law has been written on your heart.

Just as learning happens in many different ways, so also does prayer. It is important to figure out what makes prayer most effective for you. Some people keep a daily prayer journal and write down their prayers to God as well as His answers to their prayers. Keeping track of God's blessings can build your faith and encourage your prayer life.

Others find that at times life is so overwhelming that they must carefully and thoughtfully write their prayers as they work through situations. Using your mind, your hands, and your eyes to write the prayers brings intensity to what is said to God. And writing prayers can help you concentrate on what you are saying to God when you might otherwise be distracted.

worth thinking about

▶ **Writing in a** journal of prayer every day can show you not only how you are progressing in your prayer life, but also how God answers your prayers.

▶ **Written prayers** can look like poetry or like the lyrics from songs. Your prayers reflect who you are and how you are made.

▶ **Precious memories** come from looking back at times in your life when God was particularly amazing. Write and date your prayers, and keep them in a special place. This will encourage you when you need it.

> *Written prayer was critical in lengthening my attention span during prayer as well as personalizing my conversations with God.*
> Becky Tirabassi

question

Should part of prayer be listening, not talking?

It may sometimes seem that prayer is a one-sided event. But since prayer is a conversation between you and God, it is indeed two-sided. It may seem odd to think of God, whom you cannot see, carrying on His end of a conversation, but the relationship He wants with you is dynamic. He desires to have a vital relationship in which both of you participate. When you pray with the expectation of God's participation, eagerness enhances your prayer.

answer

There used to be an old saying in churches that God has a phone number—Jeremiah 33:3: "Call to Me, and I will answer you, and show you great and mighty things, which you do not know" (NKJV). The Bible states there and in other places that God does indeed speak to His people. When they try to picture God speaking, many people think of the movie image of Moses on the mountain when he heard the booming voice of God. But that isn't what most people experience today.

In the Old Testament particularly, the Bible does mention God speaking so that people could hear Him. But many examples exist that tell of God's impressing His words on the hearts of people, of God's speaking through the words of the Bible, or of God's causing people to think on certain things that are in line with His plans and purposes.

As you take the time to meditate on the words of the Bible, you gain a deeper understanding of God. And with it, you gain a better grasp of His ways. When reading the Bible, God can speak to you through what stands out or comes to your attention. He gives you wisdom on how to pray His way. Sometimes you can sense His side of the conversation best if you sit quietly and let His presence come. God is sovereign, and He has always made Himself known to His people.

worth thinking about

▶ **When you listen** to someone, you show respect with your attention. God deserves no less.

▶ **If you spend** all your time talking, you do not benefit from God's side of your relationship. God will communicate His love to you if you give Him a chance.

▶ **Silence also creates** a place where the Bible is savored and treasured. By thinking on a passage from the Bible during a quiet time, you can see things you have never seen before.

When we purposefully pray to be sensitive to His Spirit, we will be amazed at how He guides us and at the "coincidences" in which we find ourselves able to encourage others in their walk with God!

Debbie Williams

question

▼

How can you pray when you have no words left?

There comes a time when you just run out of words. You have talked to friends and family about a situation that troubles you, and you have prayed long and hard about the issue. You know that God is listening, but during the time you have waited, you have spoken every thought and laid out every argument you have for the resolution of the problem. You wonder what you could possibly add now.

answer

▼

You know how it feels to have talked about a problem so long you cannot form another sentence or even articulate what it is you need to see happen. Most people become uncomfortable with silence, and if answers to prayers that you're waiting for seem slow to come, you talk. With great affection, God knows your every weakness and habit, and, as always, He makes provision for it.

"In certain ways we are weak, but the Spirit is here to help us. For example, when we don't know what to pray for, the Spirit prays for us in ways that cannot be put into words" (Romans 8:26, CEV). This is one of the most beautiful and comforting scriptures for those who practice prayer. No matter how inadequate you feel in your prayer life, as a believer you have the Holy Spirit to make up for your weaknesses. Every prayer you start with only the words "Oh, God," the Holy Spirit finishes by filling in the blanks and letting God know what you wish you could say.

That comfort and assurance blesses anyone who prays. You know that when you reach the end of what your brain can think or your mouth can speak, you are covered. And if you have no idea what to pray about a situation, you can trust that the Holy Spirit continues the request you bring to God.

worth thinking about

▶ "Help!" is a perfectly valid and to-the-point prayer. God answers this kind of prayer as readily as any other.

▶ Much is communicated in a sigh, an expression, your body's movements, or a host of other ways. God knows what is in your heart, so you need not worry that He will not understand.

▶ Sometimes the very act of continuing to talk simply gets in the way of what you really need to communicate to God.

> *The Spirit dwelling within us prays, not in words and thoughts always, but in a breath deeper than utterance. There is real prayer according to how much there is of Christ's Spirit in us.*
>
> Andrew Murray

question

Can a song be a prayer to God?

For some people, music is a second language. These people always seem to have a song on their minds, and they hum or whistle tunes during the day. Events and thoughts are often accompanied by an appropriate song that's been chasing in the heads of musical people, and significant revelations have come through music they have heard. A natural progression of the prayer journey might be the consideration of songs and prayer.

answer

Songs often express the deepest longings or words of praise to God that are too much to merely be spoken. Miriam sang a lively song of praise to God as thanks for God parting the Red Sea and saving the Israelites from slaughter and imprisonment by the Egyptians. Many of the psalms talk about God giving a new song to sing to those who love Him. In Ephesians, believers were told to sing spiritual songs to one another.

Music played a big part in biblical history. Because it is so prominent in the stories of the Bible, you can tell that music is a valid and valuable form of communication between God and people. Over and over, music enabled people to praise God with the emotion and passion He deserved. Words alone could never express such intensity, but words mixed with the beauty and complexity of tone and rhythm carry much more meaning.

You are unique and formed just the way God intended. You may be a person with musical ability and a love for anything with a melody. If that is the case, then a most appropriate expression of your love for God, or things that are on your mind, would be in song. God created melody and music, and He created you. Such expressions from your heart could do nothing but please God.

worth thinking about

▶ **If you are** musically gifted, sharing that gift with God as you pray is like a prayer and thanksgiving at the same time.

▶ **Even if a song** is sung with enthusiasm but not with tone, God delights in it. The Bible says to make a joyful noise to the Lord. He is not a music critic.

▶ **Singing brings out** a childlike joy, or even a sadness of heart. Emotions speak out vividly when you sing, and God hears every nuance.

> *When we tie music to prayer, we have a powerful combination. Singing also adds vivacity, buoyancy, and gaiety to our prayers. You may know the old adage "the one who sings prays twice."*
>
> Richard J. Foster

Does it matter if you forget to pray every day?

Life is busy. It is rare to find people who have relaxed periods in their days. Work, school, day-care schedules, obligations at church—these things keep a twenty-four-hour day nearly full. You know you should pray, but it is really hard to carve out a time when you can sit and quietly pray each day. Life throws unexpected curve-balls, and many days disappear with your realization that you had no conscious thoughts of God that day.

answer

God understands the pace of the day. It seems things are speeding up every year, and there is always a shortage of time. You may even wish at times you were two people, and then you could get everything done. This dilemma causes distress. You may already feel you never get enough sleep, and you cannot figure out how to set aside a time when you could consistently pray each day.

The Bible says that God tells His secrets to those who respect Him (Psalm 25:14). You have His friendship when you love Him and spend time talking to Him in the way He has asked you to do. Imagine being close enough that God considers you a friend and shares His secrets with you. It is an amazing thought.

Because the life of prayer is a journey, you know you can always be aiming for something better. If you pray as you can, you are being faithful to God. If you want a much deeper and more life-sustaining relationship with Him, then you need to ask God to show you how to order your life in such a way that you can find the time to meet with Him every day. You may not be able to see where you could change your priorities, but God does. Ask for His help, and you will soon see ways you never dreamed of to find time for prayer.

worth thinking about

- ▶ If you had an admirer who very much wanted to spend time with you, it would seem easier to make the time to meet. Make time to meet with God.

- ▶ It may be helpful to schedule a time on your calendar to meet with God. Do whatever you need to do to remind yourself to pray.

- ▶ Know that eventually, those times with God will bless you so much that you will not want to miss them.

> *Prayer shouldn't be a burden but a privilege—*
> *a privilege God has graciously given us*
> *because He wants our fellowship.*
> Billy Graham

question

42

Can you pray when
you know you
are doing wrong?

When beginning a life of prayer or increasing the practice of prayer in your life, certain of your behaviors may
start to seem uncomfortable or awkward. Talking to God
freely in prayer and doing things you know are wrong
don't fit easily together into the same place in your life,
and you become uncomfortable. When that happens,
you wonder if you should talk to God about it or stop
praying at all if you offend Him.

answer

Even though it seems harsh, the Bible states that if you
are cozy with evil, God will not hear you (Psalm 66:18).
Understanding the holiness of God is difficult for
human beings, who, by nature, struggle with sin and
temptations every day. But knowing the propensity for
sin that encompasses people, you can start to think that
any unknown slipup is enough to keep God from hearing your prayers.

Because God is so loving and kind, He provides a feeling
of conscience that convicts you of sin. If He wants you to
face sin and ask forgiveness, that conviction will nudge

you repeatedly until you deal with it. You might also find that someone you respect will point out an area of difficulty in your life. The key to prayer and sin is this: if you know you are doing wrong, it is willful sin in God's eyes and will hinder your prayer life. If you go to God for forgiveness and freedom from the sin, His grace covers you as you let Him work in your life.

No one is perfect but God. People will always struggle with sin. God looks at the heart of the person who loves Him. A heart that is tender to Him and responds to the conviction of sin is a heart that brings prayers that are heard by God.

worth thinking about

▶ **Good relationships** are open and honest. If your heart is hiding sin, you cannot be open and honest with God.

▶ **One sin leads** to another, and to another. The only way to break the chain of increasing wrong in your life is to confess it to God and let Him break you free.

▶ **Ask God** each day to clean up your life. He will show you what needs to be changed, and what you must do.

> *A clean heart, or a pure, unadulterated heart, is a requirement for mountain-moving prayer. One whose heart is not clean can't enter into the intimate fellowship with the Father that He so desires.*
> Jennifer Kennedy Dean

question

▼

Must you have right motives when you pray?

When you pray, you will have times when you wonder if your frame of mind is right to be talking to God. You know He knows what you are thinking, so when you ask for something you really want, pray for neighbors you are not so fond of, or pray about a problem at work, you wonder how to tell if the way you are thinking affects your prayers.

answer

▼

The Bible overflows with wisdom and admonitions about loving God, loving others, and loving yourself. A constant theme runs through the Old and New Testaments that beckons believers to submit their sinful attitudes and behaviors to God for forgiveness and heal-ing. Unloving and self-centered behavior is sinful. God, who is perfect, cannot abide sin, and so He wants your prayers to spring from motivation that is pure.

As direct communication with God, your prayer comes best to Him if your motives are held up to the light of God's truth in the Bible and examined. By knowing His truth and praying with knowledge, love and submission to God's purposes will begin to motivate your prayers. In Romans 12 you'll find guidelines of Christian behavior, including blessing those who persecute you, loving while not being hypocritical, hating evil things, and overpowering evil with good. God wants you to become more and more like Jesus as you follow Him.

God loves a pure heart. If you wonder about the motivations behind your prayers, ask God to give you a pure heart and to free you from any motivations of the heart that do not honor Him. He will bring things to your attention that you might not even realize. Let Him help you in His gentle way, and you will know that your prayers come from a heart that is right with God.

worth thinking about

▶ Jesus said that those with pure hearts and motives would receive blessing, for they would see God.

▶ God cannot honor prayers with bad motives. That would mean God could do wrong. He will not even entertain such prayers.

▶ There is no way to fail with God. You can tell Him you know your prayer is not right, and He will graciously help you regain right attitudes. Then your prayer will be pleasing to Him.

> This is scary: You can tame a tiger, but you can't tame a tongue—it's never been done. The tongue runs wild, a wanton killer. With our tongues we bless God our Father; with the same tongues we curse the very men and women he made in his image. Curses and blessings out of the same mouth! My friends, this can't go on.
>
> James 3:7–10, THE MESSAGE

question

▼

Does God hear when you have not forgiven someone?

People can hurt one another badly. When you have been hurt, letting that hurt go can be very difficult. You know that God asks you to forgive freely, and when you have not, your prayers can even feel awkward or stifled. At the heart of your relationship with God is His loving forgiveness, so it is important to know what God says about the issue of extending forgiveness to others and your prayer life.

answer

▼

Many times in the Bible God says that just as He has freely forgiven you for whatever sins you have brought to Him, He expects you to forgive others. In Mark 11:25, Jesus said, "When you are praying, first forgive anyone you are holding a grudge against, so that your Father in heaven will forgive your sins, too" (NLT). The words are clear that anyone wanting to keep receiving God's forgiveness needs to deal with any bitterness and resentment of their own.

Unresolved conflict poisons your relationships with other people and eventually even poisons your relationship with God. Holding unforgiveness against others makes light of the undeserved grace given to you by God when He forgave your sins. Eventually, the bitterness crowds out so much of the light and love of God that it will affect the prayers you pray. It is hard to be angry or bitter and be full of faith at the same time.

No matter what it takes, be willing to forgive, and ask God for His help in letting the wrong against you go. Realize that, at times, forgiveness happens bit by bit. When offenses hurt deeply and wounds go far back in your life, it will take some time to work through them. God does not penalize you for things that take time. The important thing is that your heart is willing and that you are trying to work through it. God will bless your efforts, and He will continue to hear your prayers.

worth thinking about

▶ **Forgiveness is** a practice and a lifestyle. Realizing the depth of the sacrifice Jesus made for you will help keep offenses against you in the right balance.

▶ **Even if you** must pray more than once to be able to forgive someone, keep at it. You will reach a point of freedom from any bitterness.

▶ **Forgiveness refused** brings in bitterness that slowly and surely poisons your relationships with God and with others. Willingness to forgive any offense cuts off the cycle of bitterness and breathes health back into your life.

> *We do not wait until we feel like forgiving; we forgive by making an intentional choice, a willful decision to let a matter drop. When we do, we make a way for our prayers to be answered.*
>
> Joyce Meyer

question

Can you pray if you are not sure you believe?

A common struggle for any believer is that against doubt. Dark nights when you feel alone. Struggles that seem to have no end. Delayed answers to prayer. All these work to foster little nagging doubts that assail your brain. Is God really there, after all, and does He indeed care about the situation you are in? Even if you have been a praying person, doubt can creep into your thinking. In either case, you need to address your doubt.

answer

God invites anyone who feels he lacks faith to pray the words of one father in the Bible. The father desperately needed Jesus to heal his child, but he was honest enough to admit his doubt: "I do believe, but help me overcome my unbelief!" (Mark 9:24, NLT). That kind of raw honesty knocks the stigma away from doubt and puts it squarely where God can deal with it.

If you pray with a sincere heart, God hears and accepts even prayers that you voice with doubt. God is pleased, even though you pray with uncertainty. Having faith is a gift, and if you lack faith, God still knows what you need and will help. He will strengthen you as you struggle to trust Him.

The important thing is this: do not stop praying, even if you struggle with doubt. Be honest. Tell God exactly where your faith is right now, and ask Him to reveal any misconceptions you might have. He is faithful to show you, when the time is right, when and where you began believing that God is not absolutely trustworthy. He is completely able to change your thinking and give you strong faith. He hears you and will do it. Just keep going to Him in prayer.

worth thinking about

▶ **The best remedy** for unbelief is prayer. Ask God to give you understanding and insight. He will make things clear to you.

▶ **Faith comes** with practice in believing. One step at a time, you will believe God for more and more. Each time a prayer is answered, your faith builds.

▶ **Listen to things** that build your faith. Read things that build your faith. Do things that build your faith. Keep your mind focused on God and not on the problems in your life.

> *Faith is not believing in my own unshakable belief. Faith is believing an unshakable God when everything in me trembles and quakes.*
> Beth Moore

What if the future seems too frightening to pray about?

The future is in the hands of One who is preparing something better than eye hath seen, or ear heard, or has entered into the heart of man to conceive.

John Baillie

46

Should you pray when you do not feel like it?

Doing things when and if you want is an easy way to live life as an adult. When you do not wish to do something, you can choose not to. This way of living, though, is not helpful if you wish to cultivate a life of prayer. There are plenty of times when you do not feel like praying, and you need sufficient motivation to continue on regardless of what you feel like doing.

answer

Some years ago, an illustration many public speakers used was one that compared Christian life to the cars on a train. The engine and the cars all bore labels representing aspects of life. To work best, the engine of the train needed to bear the label of Faith, with Emotions on the cars that followed. The reasoning was that if Emotion was the engine of the train, there would be nothing to move it forward. The driving force of faith cannot follow the inward-focused emotion.

This illustration rings true. Emotions change with circumstances, and do not always reflect what you know to be truth. If left to lead, emotions would let you drift away from a true and lasting faith in God, and your prayer life would nearly disappear. There is a discipline in prayer that must be exercised, just as you have to discipline your body to exercise in order to stay healthy. Make it a regular habit.

Faith, however, remains the same, no matter what. Faith tells you that God is still God and He is infinitely concerned about your life, whether you feel like praying or not. God never changes. God says His eyes are on the faithful of the land and that He can dwell with them. As much as you can—be faithful, and ask God to increase your faith.

worth thinking about

▶ Children are not typically permitted to do things only when they want to because it would allow them to grow up selfish. God, as the perfect parent, wants you to grow up balanced and healthy spiritually.

▶ Self exerts its own will, but when you submit yourself to God and obey what He tells you, you will discover that self will diminish and you will bloom with spiritual maturity.

▶ If God is important in your life, you will make prayer a priority.

Jesus told his disciples a story about how they should keep on praying and never give up.
Luke 18:1, CEV

question

How do you overcome feeling God will not help you?

Trust in your relationships with others comes over time and with experience. If you have experienced broken trust in key relationships in your life, those broken issues can affect the confidence with which you approach God. Praying becomes labored if you have a nagging feeling that God just will not come through for you, and your efforts to keep on praying may fizzle out over time. Lack of trust must find a remedy if you are to grow in prayer. Thankfully, the remedy is in God.

answer

In Matthew 14, Jesus' disciples were crossing a rough sea at night in a boat. Jesus, walking across the dark sea, went to them in their boat. Jesus extended a hand and invited Peter to get out and meet Him. Peter did, and he found himself walking on the water until he looked down at the waves. When he looked at Jesus, he was fine. When he looked at the waves, he sank. If you look at God, your doubts become smaller. God knows every time your trust was broken by another person and what that did to your faith. He provided a way for your healing, whether physical healing, mental healing, or emotional healing. He wants your faith to grow so that you can pray and not doubt.

Part of overcoming doubt in God is to surround yourself with people and things that uplift your faith. Listen to inspiring music. Talk to other followers of God about their struggles with doubt. Read books about people who have strong, overcoming faith. Read the Bible.

"GOD-affirmers find themselves loved every time they turn around" (Psalm 32:10, THE MESSAGE). It takes only a bit of faith to believe that God understands your struggle and that He will help you and heal you as you continue to go to Him in prayer. Don't shy away! Only God can wash away the disappointments of broken relationships and hear your doubts while He sees your honest efforts to grow. Ask God to show you His faithfulness in your life.

worth thinking about

- ▶ **Keep a journal** of answered prayer or grace moments in your life. Review it often so it can build your faith.

- ▶ **Talk to people** who have been believers for a long time. You will be encouraged by their faith and by the stories of answered prayer they will share.

- ▶ **Ask God** to remove any thoughts from your past that are contrary to God's truth and that stand in the way of believing. He will bring you freedom.

Faith and doubt are needed—not as antagonists but working side by side—to take us around the unknown curve.
Lillian Smith

question

Can you pray if you do not feel close to God?

For all that is said about prayer, it can seem that prayer would be something best done by someone who is a spiritual giant, by someone who has known God closely for a long time. You hesitate, feeling that if you do not sense God's presence then He might not be able to hear your voice. At the very least, prayer can seem uncomfortable when you are not sure of His attention. So you wonder if you should pray at all.

answer

The reason for the distance felt between you and God rarely lies with God. Most often, something pulls you away from God—the cares of life, sin you struggle with, or the busyness of life cutting away at your time in prayer. Just as if you had not talked to a friend for a long time, not praying for a long time can make you feel distant from God. And that same feeling strikes when you first begin to pray.

The best news about that supposed distance is the truth that God never changes. He says that He is the same yesterday, today, and tomorrow. He also says that He stands at the door and knocks, so you know that He always wants your relationship to be closer still. He hears every cry of your heart, and even the very thoughts you think.

God is not going anywhere. He does not turn His back on you, but instead He encourages you to keep pressing into relationship with Him so you can enjoy the benefits of loving Him with your whole heart. In other words, God wants you to keep praying. How will you respond? You need not feel guilty or depressed because of the distance you feel. When you feel helpless and unsure, you can be assured that God will help you feel closer to Him.

worth thinking about

▶ **Even King David** in the Bible complained at times about not sensing God. He was called a man after God's own heart, and he enjoyed a close relationship with God. Those times did pass.

▶ **Praying is the** *only* way to get closer to God. Spending time with Him in prayer each day builds familiarity and sensitivity to God, and you will feel closer.

▶ **Even if you** do turn away from God for a time, He is always waiting and ready to welcome you back.

> *When I am tempted to complain about God's lack of presence, I remind myself that God has much more reason to complain about my lack of presence.*
>
> Philip Yancey

49

Does it matter if you are in church when you pray?

God does not give a list of specific do's and don'ts that must be accomplished in order for prayer to be effective, and so church attendance can seem to be unnecessary. Many people believe that worshiping God can happen just as effectively out in nature, and so logic would dictate that effective prayer may also be just as effective if you are not attending church. The issue really lies in the quality of your spiritual life in general.

answer

Do you want God's best, or are you satisfied with God's acceptable provision for your life? In the Bible, you see that something happens when believers spend time worshiping God and learning together. This concept is important enough that God describes believers as being the body of Christ, as being a group of people who together form one entity with God's purpose at their center.

The apostle Paul described how the body of believers in his time walked in unity, loved one another, and believed in God together. He described the gifts God gave each person to enrich and reach out to others. The result was a group of people who believed the same, supported one another, and, therefore, could accomplish God's will in their world. They would pray in agreement with one another, and it is recorded that miracles happened.

There is power in God's people when they work together and learn together the way He intended. His larger purpose in the world is accomplished in ways you cannot always understand. How much better to have a church family surrounding you when you pray and grow as a believer, with people who can help you when you feel discouraged, and who can help your faith stay strong. Church life profits you and your prayer life.

worth thinking about

▶ **When you are** by yourself, it is much harder to keep your thinking right and your faith on the mark.

▶ **No church** is perfect because churches are made up of people, but some churches may fit you better than others.

▶ **Church gives** you a place where you can learn more about your faith, about the Bible, and about how to pray more effectively and with greater joy. Those gains are difficult to get on your own.

> *Let us consider one another in order to stir up love and good works, not forsaking the assembling of ourselves together, as is the manner of some, but exhorting one another, and so much the more as you see the Day approaching.*
> Hebrews 10:24–25, NKJV

question

What do you do if there is no answer?

Prayer puts you out on a limb of faith as you pray to the God you cannot see. When you pray about matters of importance or of great need, you can feel vulnerable in your need, or anxious to receive an answer to the prayers. If an answer does not come soon, you wonder if God heard you, or if your prayer had right motivation. Second-guessing yourself or God does not build your faith, so you need to know how to stand in strong faith despite the seeming silence.

answer

Philippians 4:6 says to be anxious for nothing, advising, "Don't worry about anything; instead, pray about everything. Tell God what you need, and thank him for all he has done" (NLT). God knows how bleak life can look if you focus on the things that are unfinished, undone, and unanswered. Whispers of doubt assail your mind when you wait.

So when you pray and answers do not come quickly, the challenge is to resist the temptation to look at the problems and doubt whether God heard or cares about the issues that are important to you.

When God doesn't answer prayer the way you'd like Him to, know that your ungranted request may help you appreciate God and His gifts even more. While that may be hard to understand when waiting for God to answer, underneath that issue is faith in the truth of the Bible. These things are true—God is good, all the time, and He is working all things for your good because you love Him. Prayer involves surrendering to God's wisdom and love for you, and reminding yourself of truth whenever time passes slowly. An answer will come, in one way or another, because God is good. And whether that answer is yes, no, or wait, it is always the perfect answer that comes from a perfect God.

worth thinking about

▶ Time will best tell if what seems like a no answer is simply an answer that comes more slowly than other answers.

▶ God's timing in your life is perfect, and He knows best what events must happen before an answer comes. Be patient and expectant.

▶ An answer that takes time is even more assuredly the best answer for your life. God is not in a hurry.

> God will always come to the one who continues to submit in prayer to His will and doesn't lose heart. The provisions of God are many, and can come in a multitude of ways.
> Henry and Norman Blackaby

51

question

▼

Do you lack faith if you ask God more than once?

Many people remember a time with a child who wanted a special treat or experience and who pestered any adult nearby with the same request over and over. When asking God for something in prayer, you can begin feeling like that overexcited child, wondering just when God will become annoyed at your repetitions. Thankfully, the Bible contains examples of people going to God in prayer many times for the same thing, and God's response was one of compassionate patience rather than annoyance.

answer

▼

God openly invites asking. "Ask, and it will be given to you; seek, and you will find; knock, and it will be opened to you. For everyone who asks receives, and he who seeks finds, and to him who knocks it will be opened" (Matthew 7:7–8, NKJV). This indicates not just one form of asking, but several. God knows you have needs and expects you to trust Him enough to ask, and to ask as often as necessary.

An important distinction lies between prayers prayed as a child who fears that without constant reminders God will forget the request, and prayers prayed as a child of God who understands that waiting for answers purposefully deepens character. The ability to believe and keep praying and waiting becomes perseverance, which God values in your life. The need to keep praying can be a season when God wants you to grow deep roots of perseverance.

Repeated requests for inappropriate things will usually receive an answer of no from God. The way to avoid this is to love God with all your heart by reading the Bible and spending regular time with God in prayer. Just as a child learns to know what his parent wants for him to have, you can know what God wants for you to receive by keeping a close relationship with Him. Then, whether the answer comes now or later, you know that God cares for your needs and will not let you down.

worth thinking about

▶ **Keeping God first** in your thoughts and your desires will ensure that you are not asking God for things He prefers you not request.

▶ **You know** your needs and the reasons behind them. God knows but sees the big picture, too, and He knows what else must happen before your prayer is answered.

▶ **Just as seeds** planted in the ground take time to mature and provide fruit, sometimes you must hold on to prayers so both you and your prayers mature before the answer comes.

> *Lord, help us to understand the seasons in nature and know to wait with patience for the fruit we long for. Fill us with the assurance that you will not delay one moment longer than is needed, and that faith will yield.*
>
> Andrew Murray

question
▼

How do you know what God is saying?

Giving your concerns and needs to God represents a big step of faith. Once you cross that hurdle, your prayer life becomes easier and you have freedom to enjoy talking to God every day. But as important as it is to speak to God, listening is also important. This can seem like a much bigger hurdle to cross, and one that seems much harder to understand.

answer
▼

In the Book of John, people are compared to sheep that belong to God. God, in turn, is compared to a shepherd. In ancient times, a flock of sheep knew the voice of its shepherd because the sheep heard his voice all the time. They would not follow another voice. Like that flock of sheep, you learn the voice of your Shepherd when you spend time reading the Bible. You know what He sounds like, what He thinks, and the way He does things in your life. The greater your familiarity with the Bible, the easier you can sense what God is saying to you.

God's answers to you can come in different ways. A scripture may stand out to you that is particularly meaningful, a thought might come strongly to your mind that pertains to your prayer, circumstances may change and make a choice obvious, or a sureness may come to you about something that is not from your own thinking.

The best opportunity you have of recognizing if God is speaking to you in response to your prayers is to immerse yourself daily in the Bible. By saturating your mind with God's words and truth, you will immediately know if something you are thinking lines up with His ways. Because God never changes, knowing the Bible in your heart and mind will protect you from going astray or being misled. When you trust Him and His voice, you will know His peace.

worth thinking about

▶ **Listening for God** to speak requires that you take time to be quiet. Only then will you connect with God in a way that allows you to hear.

▶ **The comfort** of knowing God speaks as well as listens enables you to connect with Him in a real way.

▶ **Be careful** when listening for God to speak. Your own voice can sound surprisingly like an answer from Him. Hold the answer up to God's Word to evaluate.

> *When the biblical words of Jesus abide in our mind, we hear the very thoughts of the living Christ, for he is the same yesterday, today, and forever. And out of that deep listening of the heart comes the language of prayer which is a sweet incense before God's throne.*
>
> John Piper

question

▼

In what ways are prayers for direction answered?

When you do not know which choices are best or what decisions to make about important issues in your life, you want to ask God. Some decisions have lasting consequences, so knowing what God says is vital. You want to know what God's best is for you, but how can you know the best choice or decision in the situations before you? You trust God, but trusting yourself to hear and understand is a different matter.

answer

▼

The Bible states that as you trust in God with all your heart, and refuse to lean on your own understanding, He will direct your paths. One key to this lies in acknowledging God in everything you do. While this sounds simple, it means continual awareness of God throughout your day, submission to His righteousness and wisdom in every circumstance, praying often, and spending time reading the Bible.

The time spent absorbing God and His ways through reading the Bible enables Him to guide your path and clarify your decisions by the influence of His eternal truth on your life. His wisdom becomes yours, and your choices become His. As you study and learn more and more about Him, He will give you the help you need. God becomes your greatest influence, and with that, you will have His help when you need direction.

God's direction can come through a strong feeling to make one choice over another, or through situations that line up to make a decision easy. You might even find that something you read in the Bible illustrates the best choice in your circumstances. No matter how the direction comes to you, ask God to make Himself clear and give you His peace when you are choosing the right direction.

worth thinking about

▶ **The Bible says** you can have the mind of Christ. Fellowship with Him builds a unity in your thinking that makes it easier to know what God is saying to you.

▶ **A good saying** is "Follow the peace." Where you have peace, God is there. Where there is no peace, chances are it is not the right decision.

▶ **A prayer for** direction must go hand in hand with the resolve to do whatever God shows you to do.

▼

God's sovereign plans for you embrace a myriad of seemingly insignificant details. What a challenge to trust Him . . . to obey Him in everything . . . to walk in the closest fellowship with Him! Believe me, the details count!

Joni Eareckson Tada

question

▼

How long do you keep praying?

In today's fast-food, fast-paced generation, it is hard to wait for anything. Technology makes communication faster and faster, and everything from banking to ordering materials happens in an instant. Remembering to pray for a person or an issue for several days seems a long time, let alone when a situation or need stays unresolved for months. You wonder how long to keep praying or if you are even supposed to keep praying that long.

answer

▼

The Book of Luke describes the story of a poor widow who persistently went before a judge with her great need for justice from her enemy. She kept going to the judge every day until she finally got her request. That story was meant to illustrate the principle that people must always pray and never lose heart, for God works on behalf of His own, willingly and readily, much more than the judge in the story.

God asks that you pray always, and so you know it is possible to pray for as long as the need continues. The widow in the story went to an unbelieving judge. You go to your loving God. He hears you and wants to meet your needs, but there are times when God wants you to develop perseverance in prayer, and to exercise and build that character often requires prolonged prayer. A general rule for praying about something is that as long as you remember the need and feel burdened with the importance of it, you should pray about it.

A fine line of faith and doubt needs attention when you pray for your own needs in particular. If you find yourself requesting the same answer over and over, you need to search your heart to see if you actually struggle with doubt that God will provide what you need. At times like that, you may need to pray once and, believing that God heard and will care for your needs, leave the prayer with Him in faith.

worth thinking about

▶ **If God wants** you to pray for someone, you do not have to work up the desire to do it. He will let you know and cause you to remember the person.

▶ **Prayer cannot** become a good-luck ritual repeated every day. Communication with God is a relationship with the One who loves you more than you can imagine, not something to do to prevent trouble.

▶ **Prayer grows** progressively, and needs to be a continual, ever-deepening part of your life.

> *In order to be effective in prayer, it is important for us to learn to discern when to press into more fervent prayer in a situation and when to release it.*
>
> Joyce Meyer

55

How can you continue to pray for someone?

Many people struggle to produce the fortitude to keep doing something as long as it needs to be done. Prayer is no exception. It is difficult to keep praying for someone over a period of time when it appears that nothing is changing. You may run out of words to say or prayers to pray, and you may become frustrated because it looks like God is doing nothing. You want to know how to be able to keep praying for someone the way God desires.

answer

If you think of how you felt when you went through your toughest period of life, you can better understand how to pray for an extended time for someone else. God tells you to have compassion on others, and to love one another tenderheartedly as brothers and sisters. When you can empathize with the person going through hard times, you will pray with less frustration. God says to hold others in higher esteem than yourself, and to do it gladly, and this governs your prayer as well.

Colossians 4:2 states, "Pray diligently. Stay alert, with your eyes wide open in gratitude" (THE MESSAGE). Vigilance is a positive, proactive approach to continual prayer, and requires you to practice self-discipline. By loving others as your own family, you can obey God and pray earnestly and with thanksgiving. If you find it hard to love others that way, ask God for His help and grace to do it. You will find He fills your heart with a love that does not come from your own feelings.

Remind yourself of what God has done for you and of the prayers others have spoken to God for you. Learn to pray for the needs of others before you pray for your own needs, and it will become a practice and a frame of mind that will help you have the vigilance you need. Whenever you feel a strong urge to pray for someone else, take the time to do it. God is reminding you to care enough to pray.

worth thinking about

- ▶ **You cannot imagine** what your prayers may accomplish in the life of another. You may have the strength to pray when they do not, and that can make all the difference.

- ▶ **It is a** sacrifice of love to pray for a friend, even when the need goes on longer than you imagined it would.

- ▶ **God's timescale** measures differently from yours. What seems a long time to you may be only a blink of His eye.

> *Make this your common practice: Confess your sins to each other and pray for each other so that you can live together whole and healed.*
> James 5:16, THE MESSAGE

Why should you bless other people in prayer?

The happiest prayers of all are when we call down blessings on people. Send a blessing winging their way for no good reason except a sudden desire to wish them well.

Marjorie Holmes

56

question

If there is no answer, did God say no?

Waiting is hard to do. And waiting for answers to prayer is even harder. If you have needs important enough to take to God, you want to see Him care about your needs more than you do, and waiting allows you to entertain doubts about just how much He cares. When there is no obvious answer to your prayers, you wonder whether that means God said no to your need, or if He just did not hear.

answer

It has been said that God always gives one of three answers—yes, no, or wait. That is oversimplified a bit, but in essence it is true. God may answer a prayer or a need fairly quickly, and you know His grace met you where you needed it most. The harder situation is when there is apparently no answer. Does that mean God said no to the request, or are you supposed to wait? The Bible says that hope does not disappoint because the love of God has been poured out in your heart. Hope keeps you believing God.

Because of the hope you have received from knowing God and His character, you know that answers come on His timetable, not yours. Do not let yourself believe God does not hear you, or assume He will not answer you.

Practicing faith allows you to wait, knowing that God's character will not allow Him to ignore your need. The faith that gives you that hope comes from reading the Bible and soaking in God's promises.

Trusting God enables you to wait in peace. When an answer is no to a prayer, you will know in your heart that God answered. Even when you receive the answer of no, you can still experience peace from God, with a sure feeling that the matter was addressed. But if you are waiting, then realize that, at the least, the wait builds character in you. Your faith and trust in God should grow, as you keep recognizing that He knows best.

worth thinking about

▶ **Determine from the** beginning that you will wait on God. Make up your mind to wait until you get an answer before you act on things big or small.

▶ **Practicing patience** in prayer shows God you are interested in growing closer to Him and not just wanting an answer to your prayers.

▶ **If you trust** God, you trust that His answers are true and right. The answer really means less than your trust in God.

> *What would happen if God answered every prayer? By answering every possible prayer, God would in effect abdicate, turning the world over to us to run. . . . Just because he doesn't answer doesn't mean he [doesn't] care. Some of God's greatest gifts are unanswered prayers.*
>
> Philip Yancey

57

question

What if you do not like the answer God gives?

You want what you want, and you know the things you do not want. So when you receive an answer from God that you dislike, you are not sure what to do with it. Your feelings about things are so real they feel like a part of you, so to accept an answer from God that feels uncomfortable leaves you completely unsettled. How do you respond to God without denying what you feel and think about a subject?

answer

It is disappointing to wait for an answer from someone only to hear an answer you do not like. If you object, you just might hear the response "Too bad!" Thankfully, God does not answer your objections to His answers in the same fashion. He knows the feelings you have in your heart, so your disappointment comes as no surprise to Him, and it does not threaten His decisions.

The comparison of a parent and a child must have been in God's mind when He inspired the verse found in Hebrews 12:11: "Now no chastening seems to be joyful for the present, but painful; nevertheless, afterward it yields the peaceable fruit of righteousness to those who have been trained by it" (NKJV). No child enjoys receiving unfavorable answers, just as you are not happy with some of the answers God gives you. But in both cases, blessings come when you accept what God has for you.

Very important is the understanding that you do not know what is best for your life. Only God, who carefully designed you and the life you lead, can know what will be best for you in any circumstance. Because God cares about anything that concerns you, He does care about your frustrations. You can freely admit them to Him in prayer, and arrive at the place of relinquishing those feelings to Him in exchange for acknowledging His perfect will. If you can reach that place, you will see that those unpleasant answers actually worked God's transformation and growth into your life.

worth thinking about

▶ You may be reluctant to liken yourself to a child, but the relationship of a parent to a child is one of the strongest bonds. Your relationship with God, your heavenly Father, is even stronger.

▶ It is tempting to respond to answers you do not like with anger or refusal to talk to God for a while, but He's wise to the ways of His children.

▶ If you write down the answers from God that you do not like, you can look back later and see why God said no. Chances are, the reasons for His answers will be both apparent and surprising.

> *If we trust in the sovereignty of God, we wrestle our way to peace in the knowledge that if an answer is for our highest good, the God who loves us will not withhold it.*
>
> Lana Bateman

58

question

Can you have a conversation with God?

A conversation consists of spoken communication that goes both ways. Maybe you never considered that prayer could be in the form of a conversation. That may seem too informal when you think of God. When you spend time together and speak with a close friend, you call that communication a conversation, and it implies a freedom and ease in your relationship as well as trust. Does prayer reach that level of familiarity considered conversation?

answer

The Bible states that God is very compassionate, and that because of His tender mercy, the sheer number of His thoughts toward you cannot be counted. You are completely familiar in all your ways to God, and you are on His mind all the time. He even knows how many hairs are on your head. The familiarity required for conversation already exists on God's side.

You may think you cannot become this familiar with God, but you can. When you read the Bible daily, His words, thoughts, characteristics, and desires pour into your heart and mind. Soon your thoughts and desires become like His, and you know Him more and more. When you pray, you connect with God in deeper ways over time, and your prayers become more like statements uttered to a good friend. Prayer is never static. You progress to deeper places if you are faithful to live a lifestyle of prayer every day.

As in any friendship, a conversation will always have comfortable lulls when you simply enjoy each other's presence. Mature prayer is the same way. You will have sweet lulls in your "conversation" when you sense God's presence and even His thoughts toward you, but you will not feel an urge to fill the silence with words. The more you pray and the more you are a student of the Bible, the more your prayer life will be like a conversation between beloved friends.

worth thinking about

▶ **You cannot** hold a conversation with God if you are afraid of what you will hear. Tell God your fears, and let Him change your thinking.

▶ **God waits** for intimate communion with you. Formal and repeated prayers can replace the intimacy with ritual.

▶ **Let your conversation** skills with God grow over time. Give yourself enough time and quiet to practice.

> *God is our best friend. We are His dear companions. And when two good friends get together for fellowship, the time spent together is rich with love, sharing, and refreshment.*
>
> Nick Harrison

question

Does God speak only through the Bible?

People say that they hear from God as though they just spoke to Him face-to-face. When you are praying, you want to know how you can hear from God. After all, you pour out your heart when you speak to God, and those things on your mind beg to be addressed by One who cares for you. The Bible says that God never changes, but you want to know if that means He still speaks as He did in ancient days.

answer

In Bible accounts, God talked to man through His actual voice, through a person's heart, and through dreams and visions. Before Jesus came and lived on earth, this was a way people learned what God wanted them to know, and they received guidance and correction that way. Some stories describe God's leading people by pillars of fire and clouds. This was unmistakable guidance!

Once Jesus came and lived on the earth, He became the embodiment of God's promises. Jesus taught people through example, words, and parables, which were recorded in the Bible. God speaks to you by His recorded words, which are divinely empowered and bring life and truth to you that will change your life.

When Jesus went back to be with God after His resurrection, He left the Holy Spirit for His people. He called the Holy Spirit the Comforter, and said He would not leave people alone. John 16:13 states, "The Spirit shows what is true and will come and guide you into the full truth. The Spirit doesn't speak on his own. He will tell you only what he has heard from me, and he will let you know what is going to happen" (CEV). Just as God chose methods to communicate with people in ancient times, He chooses methods to speak now through the Holy Spirit. By leaving the method up to God, you can trust that He will speak to you, whether through the Bible, circumstances, or your own thoughts.

worth thinking about

▶ **God cannot** be limited, so why try to limit the ways He communicates with you? If your eyes and heart are open to Him, He will surprise you in delightful ways.

▶ **Nothing that you** hear from God can ever contradict the Bible. That is a good check for you to use on what you hear.

▶ **Rely on** the Bible as your primary guide and communication manual. With it, you will be familiar with God's ways and thoughts.

Scripture teaches us that God sometimes answers our prayers by allowing things to become much worse before they become better. He may sometimes do the opposite of what we anticipate.

Cynthia Heald

question

How do you
know to pray what
God wants?

When you talk to God, you want to make sure that you know how to pray the way He wants. Being human, you know that it is easy to pray for things the way you think they should be, but you realize that sometimes your prayers may not be what God intended. You know that God knows best what situations and people need, so the question is how to find out what He wants.

answer

The simplest answer to the question of how to know the way God wants you to pray is just this: know God. The more you read the Bible and pray, the more you learn to know God and His characteristics. The Bible gives you His words, promises, and truths, and as they become part of you because of the time you spend reading and reflecting on those words, you become able to recognize when your prayers are in harmony with the values and objectives God has for people.

The next-simplest answer to the question is this: ask God. God says in the Bible to ask for anything you need, so if you need to know how to pray, ask Him. When you do, you will find that different ways to pray will come to your mind and you will know how to pray for each person or situation with which you are concerned.

Colossians 1:9 states, "We... do not cease to pray for you, and to ask that you may be filled with the knowledge of His will in all wisdom and spiritual understanding" (NKJV). God already has a plan in place to provide you with any wisdom you need. If you ask, He will provide it out of His mercy and grace toward you. If you bring yourself in line with His will for your prayer life, you will see more of God's power because you are praying His way.

worth thinking about

▶ **God knows best.** Do not underestimate the value of asking God first how to pray. He will give you the words you need.

▶ **If you know** the Bible, you have a good idea what God's will is for many circumstances. Reading the Bible every day helps you pray more effectively.

▶ **Rid your heart** of self-centered motivations or bad thoughts about others. Take them to God, and ask to be freed from them so your prayer will be pure before God.

> *God is great and mighty; there is no situation that He cannot use for good as we pray and trust Him. We dare not pray the way we want to, but as we are led by the Holy Spirit.*
>
> Joyce Meyer

question

Is there a way to know what to pray?

Not only do you need to know how to pray God's way, you also need to know what to pray. It is easy to be at a loss for words when praying, but God offers plenty of help in the Bible concerning what to pray. Finding what ideas for prayer seem right for you may seem a daunting task, but God gives you the help to find what you need and what needs to be prayed.

answer

In the Book of Ephesians, Paul encouraged people to walk worthy of their calling by becoming like Jesus, and by knowing the one Spirit, one Lord, one faith, one God and Father of all. He realized the value of centering your thoughts on God's nature, and allowing God to saturate your nature until it becomes like His. In this way, you live and think like Him, and knowing what to pray becomes as natural as breathing. Another way of describing this transformation is "falling in love" with God. When you are in love, you long to be with and to be like your loved one. You begin speaking alike and thinking alike because of the time you spend together. So it is with God.

Another way to approach knowing what to pray is realizing that God always waits for the chance to give you what you need. If you need to know how to pray, He will inspire you. If you ask Him what things in your life need His touch, He will show you. If you cannot understand what to pray for a friend, He will tell you.

The words in the Bible also show you what to pray by example, through stories of people just like you, and through the teachings of Jesus. As you read, you will find many passages that bring to mind things you want to pray. These inspirations will come to you fresh each day because God's words usher in God's power as you read, believe, and pray them.

worth thinking about

▶ **Pray with the** Spirit and pray with your understanding. Let God direct your thoughts through the Holy Spirit when you pray.

▶ **The more you** pray, the more you know to pray. Over time, the flow of God's Spirit and your prayer life become closer and more united, and prayer will flow easier.

▶ **Do not forget** to ask people what they would like you to pray for—people generally have a good idea of what they need from God.

> *Our prayers must be vital, fresh, and living. . . .*
> *Leave the dry lifeless prayers by the wayside.*
> Nick Harrison

62 question

What happens if you pray the wrong way?

You know that God is mighty and powerful. You know He is always right, and that He cannot tolerate evil. That knowledge can create a tension and a worry that you must be careful when you pray. You do not want to offend God or do the wrong thing when you are talking to Him. If you worry enough, you may even find it hard to pray at all. You know God wants a relationship with you without strain, so you need to know how to pray without fear of praying the wrong way.

answer

Even though God is all-powerful and cannot tolerate evil, you must know and believe a very important truth—you cannot override God's wisdom and rightness in any situation. He is God, and He rules over the entire universe. Even if you don't pray the way He wants, you cannot make God do anything that is wrong. It is impossible. The Bible states it this way: "How can I know all the sins lurking in my heart? Cleanse me from these hidden faults" (Psalm 19:12, NLT). Your mistakes will not take God by surprise.

If, however, you pray willingly that bad things would come to someone, or pray from the motivation of anger or vengeance, then God will deal with those wrong attitudes and sinful prayers. Purposeful sinning brings His punishment. This differs from the times you honestly make mistakes. God extends mercy to those who do what they do not intend to do.

The best way to feel at ease when you pray is to have a humble heart that is open to God, as David did in ancient times. In the Psalms, David often penned his earnest plea that God would cause him to have a clean heart. He asked God before he had reason to, and believed that when he asked, God would honor his request and deliver him from his sinful ways. Modeling that behavior gives you a pattern of prayer that will help you stay pure in the attitudes of your heart.

worth thinking about

- ▶ **Every prayer** rests upon people's faith in God's pardoning grace. If God dealt with people according to their sins, not one prayer would be heard.

- ▶ **God's grace** to you is your safety net of prayer. He is motivated by grace and moved by love for you, so He is ready to help you past any mistakes.

- ▶ **Anyone who** truly desires to spend time with God in prayer every day is not likely to pray many wrong prayers.

> *"My thoughts are nothing like your thoughts,"* says the LORD. *"And my ways are far beyond anything you could imagine."*
> Isaiah 55:8, NLT

63 question

How do you know when to stop praying for someone?

When you feel the urge to pray for someone, you pray with great enthusiasm. You know you heard the prompting of God to pray for them, and you believe He will meet the person's needs. After some time, however, you begin to wonder just how long to keep praying for the same person. You may not see a change in the circumstances. Knowing when to stop praying is harder to discern, but you do not want to stop too soon.

answer

If God brings to mind someone for whom you are to pray, He certainly knows how long He wants you to pray for the person. As a matter of habit, if you will take time to quiet yourself before God before you even start to pray, you give God the chance to bring to your mind people and things He wants you to address. While you can pray for people and situations that are already on your mind, you can also be led by God's inner prompting.

As you pray for someone, you may see the situation resolve and think that means the need for prayer is gone. That may be true, but be sure to ask God if you should keep praying. Sometimes the greatest need for God's power and hope lies in the inner life of a person after a crisis is resolved.

In His faithfulness, God will let you know if you should keep praying, even if you are not sure the need still exists. No compulsive and legalistic drive to pray should compel your prayer life. No benefit comes from endurance praying of your own initiative. Prayer rolls more like the flow of a stream, up and down, bending this way or that, but always constant and alive. Prayer for a particular person can go on until God gives you peace and a release from that concern. That is a sure sign that the flow of your prayers can be redirected.

worth thinking about

► **Know yourself** well enough to discern if you have stopped praying for someone because God released you from the need to pray, or if you just did not want to pray any longer.

► **If you misunderstand** when to stop praying, God's grace will be sufficient to cover your error. Fear should never prompt prayer.

► **Keep in mind** that praying for others is a privilege. Bringing the concerns of others to God for consideration is important work in His kingdom.

If God gives you an assignment to pray for someone or something, you will not have to "try" to work up a desire to pray; you will find that you cannot help yourself. You find yourself praying for them without even consciously planning to do so.

Joyce Meyer

64

question

What if the Bible does not give an example of prayer for your situation?

Sometimes you know what to pray. Other times, the way to pray for yourself or for other people is not as clear to you. When you read the Bible, you do not see examples of the way to pray about a particular situation, so how can you be sure to pray the way God wants?

answer

There may not be one specific verse that applies to the situation you're praying about. Just as a parent teaches her child in a broad sense rather than giving the child many specific rules to follow, God gives many broad truths in the Bible that you can apply to your life and your prayers. While there are some scriptures, especially in the Book of Proverbs, that lay out specific issues to pray about, you can also encounter many modern situations not specified in the Bible. For instance, you know through scripture that kindness and forgiveness toward those who hurt you is something God wants in your life, but the Bible does not address whether certain video games are acceptable.

God's wisdom also speaks through the lives of others. When you read or hear about the struggles of other people, you can often find God's truth and a direction to pray. When you ask God for help to know how to pray, you may find yourself drawn to books written by spiritual greats from the past or followers of God today who have faced similar circumstances. To see how someone else has prayed and been led by God can be a great encouragement to you.

You are wise if you seek out mature believers who can pray for you and advise you if you still cannot understand how to pray about a situation. Many people have experienced the same problems and have found God's way through them. You can learn much from the wisdom of others.

Ask God how to pray. This puts you in line with His thoughts when you begin, and the way to pray may become obvious to you.

worth thinking about

▶ **It is better** to surrender your thoughts and your wishes to God before you follow your own will and not His when you pray.

▶ **God's words** found in the Bible give guidance and wisdom to your prayers.

▶ **Read the Bible** before you start to pray, and you will find help and direction.

> *The LORD God is waiting to show how kind he is and to have pity on you. The LORD always does right; he blesses those who trust him.*
> Isaiah 30:18, CEV

65

Is it wrong to pray for what you think should happen?

It is hard to sort out the prayers God wants you to pray from the prayers that you think should be prayed. Certain solutions seem to make more sense, and wanting good results is only natural. You want the best for the people you care about, and that caring is expressed through your prayers. You want to know if you can pray for people's problems to be resolved in the way you think would be best.

answer

The Book of Proverbs states that there is a way that seems harmless enough, but leads to trouble. The opinions of people can be wrong compared to the perfect wisdom of God. The best way to be sure is to hold your opinions about a matter up to God's truth and see how they line up. Check your motives. You cannot see all the options or end results, so you need to make sure you agree with God. His will is perfect because His understanding is perfect. What you are thinking just may not be right.

Any time your reasoning bumps up against God's will, you have to pull back and look at your opinion and God's words again. Your motivation might be what you genuinely think is best for someone, and your words spring from compassion, but you must remember that God moves with more love and compassion than can be imagined.

Share your feelings about the situation with God because He cares, but have the attitude of yielding to His perfect will. Pray with openness to God's changing your mind. It would be wrong to pray in a way that you know God does not want, but if you pray honestly and with the knowledge that God's way is best, you will be praying the best way. Realize that God knows your desire to rescue people from their tough predicaments, but take that desire to God and ask Him to rescue them. The tough situation might have God's stamp of approval to do a deep and more complete work in their lives to build their faith and character.

worth thinking about

- ▶ **Stop to consider** this: if you were experiencing a difficult time, would you really want to pray for only your own ideas of a solution?

- ▶ **No situation exists** for which God does not already have a plan to resolve it. He looks forward to helping you see things His way.

- ▶ **God does not** ask you to quit using your brain when you pray. He asks you to acquiesce to His will.

> *How do you know what your life will be like tomorrow? Your life is like the morning fog—it's here a little while, then it's gone. What you ought to say is, "If the Lord wants us to, we will live and do this or that."*
>
> James 4:14–15, NLT

▼

How is it possible to pray through terrible heartache?

▼

The first step is to cry, shout,
let it out—until He tells you "Let
it go." . . . Lean upon God's
comforting presence as you lament
and purge your heart of the pain.
You will go on; you will learn
to forget the pain!

Dan Willis

question

How do you know if your prayers are selfish?

You know you need to pray with the right heart and the right motivation. You realize how easy it is to go to God with your own agenda, and you want to avoid this pitfall when you pray. Most troubling is the idea of prayers that come from selfish desires, because you know that everything God represents embodies selflessness. Pleasing God and seeing your prayers answered requires the same attribute.

answer

Prayer shows a progression in your relationship with God. As you grow to know God more, your prayers will become less about yourself and more about what God wants. That is a natural pattern of change accompanying spiritual maturity, if you present yourself to God continually for the conviction of sin in your life. By willingly accepting and confessing sin as revealed by God, transformation from selfishness to selflessness will occur.

The Bible contrasts the evils of self with the good found in the character of God and in the lives of believers. As you see and believe God's truth, the differences between self and good become more and more obvious. Reading the Bible and letting God teach you will sensitize you and show you what to avoid.

If you hold your prayers up to the light of God's truth, you can see if they are based on motivations of selfishness. God's words are a plumb line that serves as the measure of good and evil. Without His incomparable wisdom, you cannot identify what pleases God and what serves yourself. But in His endless mercy, you can always find forgiveness and the power to change. If you are concerned about your prayer life, ask God to reveal anything that displeases Him. He will show you, and He will show you also the way to change.

worth thinking about

▶ The Bible advises you to think on things that are true, noble, pure, and virtuous. The things you read or listen to can affect your ability to spot selfish motivations. Keep the truth of God in front of you, and stories of people with virtue.

▶ If you lack peace in your prayer life, in your family, and in your dealings with others, you may be praying from a self-centered place. Praying God's way brings peace.

▶ If you can gladly tell God that you accept His way, then your heart is putting self to the side.

> *Wherever there is jealousy and selfish ambition, there you will find disorder and evil of every kind. But the wisdom from above is first of all pure. It is also peace loving, gentle at all times, and willing to yield to others.*
>
> James 3:16–17, NLT

67

Can you pray with others if you don't agree on how to pray?

There are times when you desire to bring a need to God, but you are aware that others are praying for a different need altogether. You may also experience praying for someone but disagreeing with the need the person describes to you. In either case, you wonder if your prayers are on the mark or if you are seriously missing something. You want to know how to proceed if what you feel you must pray and what others feel they must pray do not match.

answer

The one certainty in this issue is that God sees everything, and while you know your view is finite, you also know that God is aware of not only the outcome of the situation, but also of how the person will move through it. Your specific prayers do not move God's actions like a puppeteer pulling strings. God knows everything and understands everything, and He knows how to heal and resolve problems involving even the toughest circumstances.

Knowing you do not bear the responsibility of ensuring that human needs are met is a great relief. But your prayers do matter. In the Bible, God repeatedly tells you to pray for others, and the understanding is that you share somehow in His beneficial action for others. You cry out to God for the needs of others, and you agree with God's goodness and faithfulness for them. Somehow that modest contribution helps God's work.

So if you believe you must pray for someone, be sensitive to the promptings God gives you. Ask Him if you are praying in a way that pleases Him. You may be lifting up to God one part of the situation, while another person may be praying about another part of the same situation. And you know that you can always pray scripture for the person in difficulty and the difficulty itself. Everyone going through tough times needs God's strength, wisdom, understanding, and His blessings.

worth thinking about

▶ **Just as there** are two sides to a coin, there are at least two sides to every situation. Pray as God leads you. That is your responsibility.

▶ **There are times** when you need to agree on what you are praying. If you pray for someone with another person, the two of you should agree on what to ask God.

▶ **There is power** in unity. Either be in agreement with God, or be in agreement with others who are praying. Either way, God's power will meet you.

> *Never limit God. Give Him room. Though God may seem momentarily to be moving in a direction that alarms you, He will make it work for good.*
>
> Nick Harrison

68

Doesn't the Bible say to pray in secret?

You are familiar with verses in the Bible that say you should pray in secret, but at church or in gatherings of believers, people pray aloud. You wonder if that is right to do in light of the fact that the Bible says to pray by yourself. Moreover, it seems uncomfortable to pray in front of others. You want to know how to pray in ways that work for you and also please God.

answer

In the Book of Matthew, Jesus does say to go to your room, shut the door, and pray to your Father, who is in the secret place. This passage follows the example of a man praying loud prayers in public to make himself seem important. Jesus told His followers that prayer should be given with the right attitude of humility and should start in private, with just you and God.

As with so many aspects of your spiritual life, the motivation of your heart is key to prayer. No prayer that pleases God can be self-aggrandizing or full of pride It can't have a holier-than-thou attitude. When you pray in public with others, you need to be honestly seeking God's will for that group, and to be in unity with other believers.

As your prayer life blooms from much time spent in your private place of prayer in humble yielding to God, you will more easily avoid the pitfalls of self-importance and pride when you pray aloud with others.

If you ask God continually to search your heart for any wrong motivations, He will do it, and you can confess those motivations to Him and ask to be freed from their hold. If you ask God for this help, He will help you shake free from wrongful pride and help you find and appreciate humility in your spiritual life. That attitude of always holding yourself up to God's light is one that pleases Him and leads to prayer that is healthy and right.

worth thinking about

▶ Whatever it takes to remove any pride or arrogance, it is well worth the discomfort to know that you are praying as God desires.

▶ The condition of your prayer life is dependent on the amount of time you spend praying in your own quiet place. That is where the deepest and most rewarding relationship with God is built, not when praying in groups of people.

▶ Cherish your time in secret, and protect the time and space you need to meet with God. Make this a priority in your life.

> *Prayer must be a holy exercise,*
> *untainted by vanity or pride.*
> E. M. Bounds

question

How do you pray for people who are sick?

Sickness or illness is one of the most moving conditions of the people around you. Someone suffering with pain or disease needs relief, and your heart is moved to bring that dire need to God. You want to know how to pray for those who are suffering and hurting, and how best to ask God for healing. You also want to know God's position on healing so that you are praying according to His will.

answer

Psalm 103 lists the things God provided for you, and in the list is the provision for the healing of all your diseases. When Jesus died on the cross, He paid the price for sin and sickness and so took away its power to ruin your life. The apostle Paul wrote that he wanted the people around him to prosper and be in good health even as their souls prospered. He understood that the finished work of the cross included healing and the health of the soul. It is God's will that people be healed, so you can pray with the confidence and faith that eventually, in some way, God will heal.

Healing comes in different ways and in God's timing. God heals hearts, minds, and bodies. Each person needs something unique from God, and you do not have to know how God intends to heal to be able to pray. As in other prayers, you need to ask God what to pray. It may be that God will lead you to pray for His strength and comfort.

You need not give the person practical advice unless you believe God is strongly urging you to do that. What people need is the power of God, and the working out of the healing already provided. God may heal one person quickly, while another person may go through surgery or other treatment. The outcome of prayers for healing do not reflect small faith or faulty prayers. Ask for God's perfect will to be done, and the healing will follow.

worth thinking about

▶ **Pray for those** who are sick with great compassion and sensitivity. Those people who are sick or in pain feel vulnerable.

▶ **Some people pray** for another person with their hands resting on the person's shoulders or head. If you want to do that, it is always good to ask first.

▶ **Prayer for the sick** can be as specific as addressing the exact illness, or as general as asking for God's healing and blessings of comfort. God knows what needs to be done.

> *Are any of you sick? You should call for the elders of the church to come and pray over you, anointing you with oil in the name of the Lord. Such a prayer offered in faith will heal the sick, and the Lord will make you well.*
>
> James 5:14–15, NLT

question

How do you know what God wants for the sick and suffering?

When you pray for someone who is sick or suffering from an illness, there are times when the person does not recover right away. Of all prayers, the wait is hardest for answers to prayers for those who are suffering. You wonder why God allows sickness and pain to persist, and you wonder what to continue to pray. What purpose could God have for allowing suffering to go on?

answer

Whether you pray with others or you pray alone, you benefit when you can read the Bible before you pray because it prepares you to pray according to God's will. When you pray for people who are sick or suffering, you need to be sure that you stand grounded in God's truth and are prepared to ask God to lead your prayer.

Responding to the frustration of someone waiting for healing and relief from pain brings out the urge to give reasoning and justification for the delay of God's response, but you must keep your focus on the perfect will of God and His incredible mercy and love. God does not bring pain purposefully into the lives of people, but

He uses those circumstances to bring good. God's specialty is taking anything the devil meant for harm and turning it around to bring good into people's lives and to bring glory to Himself.

God may be asking you to help the one suffering to hang on to hope. You can pray with faith and encourage them in the goodness of God. He may be working through the suffering to build up character and maturity, and you can bless that work by praying for His perfect will. And He may desire that you pray for His strength and comfort, and that the suffering one have the endurance to see God's healing. No matter what His purpose, God will show you how to pray if you ask Him.

worth thinking about

▶ **Resist the urge** to offer medical advice when you are praying for someone who is sick. Talk to the person later about practical matters, but keep prayer time connected to God.

▶ **Always encourage** the faith of those for whom you pray. If you express doubt, it will make a hard situation even more difficult.

▶ **Believe that God's love** rules over every circumstance. Your confidence in the love of God pours out through your prayers.

> *Listen for GOD's voice in everything you do, everywhere you go; he's the one who will keep you on track.*
> Proverbs 3:6, THE MESSAGE

question

How do you pray for very complicated situations?

When asked to pray for others, there are situations that seem so incredibly complex or emotionally volatile that you are not sure how to pray. When you think about those situations, you start to imagine all the ways they could be resolved and what possible consequences each resolution might bring. Because you cannot imagine the best solution out of all the possibilities, you find yourself wondering just how to pray.

answer

The good news is that you do not have to sort out the problems of others before you pray for them. Even though it follows human nature to want to solve problems and rescue those you care about, God does not expect you to know the way to solve complex or even simple situations before you pray. The act of prayer brings those problems to God and asks Him to solve them in His perfect wisdom and perfect will.

Whenever you focus on the problems that surround people, you lose the idea of the all-encompassing power of God and His overwhelming desire to help His people. Focusing on the problems actually crowds out the confidence that comes through faith in God, and the issues look larger and larger. Nothing is as bleak as a view filled with problems and heartbreak.

No matter how difficult or long-lasting the problems, God knows the stresses and damaged emotions involved. He knows the pain and the struggles behind the issues for every person. And He knows the way out or the way through the situation that is perfect. You don't have to know how to resolve the problems you bring to God. Leave behind the need to fix things. Asking for God's help is a most noble prayer, and one that He delights to answer.

worth thinking about

▶ **Pray and trust** God for difficult situations, but also be sensitive to times when you can offer practical help and support.

▶ **If you tell** someone you will pray for a tough circumstance, pray! Be true to your word and remember your promise with as much priority as if the need were yours.

▶ **No situation** is too complex for God. He knows the way through and the good He will bring from it.

> *If you have the gift of speaking, preach God's message. If you have the gift of helping others, do it with the strength that God supplies. Everything should be done in a way that will bring honor to God because of Jesus Christ, who is glorious and powerful forever.*
>
> 1 Peter 4:11, CEV

72 question

What's a good way to remember whom to pray for?

If you took the time to write down every person you cared about, the list would be very long. If you decided to pray for each person on the list, it might take hours. Because it is not possible to pray for everyone you know, how do you decide who needs prayer, and how do you remember which people you chose? When it is difficult to find the time to pray every day, it is also difficult to remember which people to lift up in prayer.

answer

First, understand the importance of prayer in the lives of others. Your prayers may be the only prayers going to God on their behalf. Jesus cared deeply for people and gave instructions to remember people with compassion by carrying their needs to God in prayer. With a tender heart motivated by love, you will find it easier to remember to pray for others each day.

To narrow down the list of people for whom to pray, ask God to bring to your mind those who most need prayer each day. He is faithful, and because His knowledge is infinite and complete, He knows which people need your prayer and intercession. If you pause when you are praying and give God a chance to bring people to your mind, you will find it becomes a revolving list of sometimes surprising names.

Once you have identified the people you are to pray for, you can help your own memory by making a list to keep near your Bible. When you pray each day, use the list for those you know need prayer for a few days or even weeks. You might benefit from listing your family members, pastors, and leaders in writing so you can remember to pray for them every day. Let God lead you and bring people to your mind, but also remember the impact your prayers may have in someone's life.

worth thinking about

▶ **Be careful** that a list of people to pray for does not become an overwhelming task you dread. Ask God which people to pray for each day.

▶ **You can pray** for others as they come to mind throughout the day. A short prayer asking God's blessings is just as important as longer prayers.

▶ **You can keep** photos in a small notebook to help focus prayers, particularly for family members. Organize your list to fit your style of prayer.

People are to be cared for, sympathized with, and prayed for, because sympathy, pity, compassion, and care accompany and precede prayer for people.

E. M. Bounds

73

question

Should you pray
for your pastor?

Praying for your pastor may slip your mind because you presume such spiritual maturity means the pastor has no needs. That is far from the truth. Your pastor stands on the front line, leading a congregation to God. Managing a large group of people brings challenges, and when you add leading their spiritual lives, the job is quite daunting. Your pastor is called to ministry, just as others are called to other places, but needs frequent prayer because of the nature of the job.

answer

God holds spiritual leaders to a higher standard than those who do not lead, because, like shepherds, they are responsible for their flocks. At the same time, they need prayers to strengthen and protect them, because they are standing out in front of their flocks in the line of defense. As modern-day shepherds, pastors do not battle actual wolves and bears, but the forces assigned to discourage and mislead believers are just as real.

The Book of 1 Timothy lists qualifications for overseers and deacons of the church, and these are good qualities to pray for in pastors. The pastor of your church needs to have godly wisdom and an ever-intimate relationship with the Lord. Your pastor needs prayers to live a righteous life of integrity in a world that offers temptations and distractions. The Bible states that a good reputation should be a hallmark of a leader of the church.

Pastors and their families are continually in front of many people, and the pressure and vulnerability can be difficult. You can pray for their strength and unity. Pray that marriages stay strong and children grow in spiritual maturity and responsibility. Pray, too, that the church be led in God's perfect will and purpose, and that the enemy's efforts to bring division and strife into the congregation be thwarted. Bring your pastor to God regularly, and pray for the refreshing of God's love to make it possible for your pastor to obey God and lead your church.

worth thinking about

▶ **Heard in a sermon**—you have the pastor you pray for. Think before you criticize. Have you prayed for your pastor this week?

▶ **The devil would** love to ruin churches, and a good place to start is the pastor. Pray for your pastor's protection.

▶ **Practical encouragement** for the pastor and the pastor's spouse can strengthen them for the difficult job they do for God.

Every Christian must testify to the truth of God, but when it comes to the call to preach, there must be the agonizing grip of God's hand on you—your life is in the grip of God for that very purpose. How many of us are held like that?
Oswald Chambers

question

Do you need to pray for politicians and leaders?

Nothing divides opinions as much as politics. The topic seems fraught with strong emotion and equally strong opinions. It is very tempting to avoid praying for politicians and leaders who do not share your view, and it is difficult to know how to pray for those leaders if you do decide to pray. Because they are people, you can guess that they must need prayer, but you may not feel qualified to pray on their behalf.

answer

You can certainly pray for leaders any prayer you would pray for other people, including prayers for God to be present in their lives, and for them to know the hope that rests in belief in God, who brings light to every situation. You can pray for their safety and their wisdom in discharging the duties of their positions.

The Book of Romans contains a startling scripture: "Obey the rulers who have authority over you. Only God can give authority to anyone, and he puts these rulers in their places of power" (13:1, CEV). No matter who is in charge, God allowed him to be in that position of authority. A person in authority needs God's wisdom to make decisions. If you do not agree with his politics, he still needs God's help. It is hard to put aside your opinions, but God says to pray for that person.

God has no political leaning or favorite. God does, however, have His perfect will that He desires for every nation and country. The decisions made by world leaders affect people groups and families. Politics affect poverty and wealth across the world. But God's plans and purposes can be accomplished through leaders of every belief and political view, and He is bigger than any agenda thought up by people. A perfect prayer for politicians and leaders of the world is for God's will to be done.

worth thinking about

▶ Understanding the news and your government will help you pray more specifically. Know what you believe, and know what you pray.

▶ Understanding and passing on your knowledge of our government's rules and operation will help your children pray as responsible citizens.

▶ Be able to see God's perfect will, even in the world of politics. Not even these leaders are outside the realm of what God controls.

> I exhort first of all that supplications, prayers, intercessions, and giving of thanks be made for all men, for kings and all who are in authority, that we may lead a quiet and peaceable life in all godliness and reverence.
>
> 1 Timothy 2:1–2, NKJV

question

How do you pray for someone to come to faith in God?

The decision to trust in Jesus for salvation is one of eternal consequences. You want those you know and those you meet to believe Jesus and have life eternally with Him in heaven, but you need to know how to pray for them to help them make the right decision. When you think of leading someone through that decision, your mind blanks and you are not sure what to do, let alone how to pray for them.

answer

The first thing to remember is that a person's salvation is most definitely God's will. The Bible even states that it is God's will that no one be lost, but all be saved. Bringing people to faith in God is really His business at the most basic level, and the business that He does best. It is only through the drawing of the Holy Spirit that people are able to receive the message of salvation. Prayer for receptive hearts and minds brings people to a place of hearing what God is saying.

Remember your own story of coming to faith in God, and pray that circumstances work to ready people, and that sharing of relevant faith stories comes at the right time. Be willing to pray and ask God to prompt you to share your story if it is His will. Pray that He will give you confidence at the right time and words to share.

Using words from the Bible helps when you pray with someone who wants to follow God. You can pray the verse Romans 10:9, that he would confess with his mouth and believe in his heart that God has raised Him (Christ) from the dead . . . and that he will be saved. You can also pray the words of John 3:16 using the person's name: God so loved the world that [person's name], who believes in Him, will not perish, but have eternal life. God honors His own words when used in prayer.

worth thinking about

▶ **Pray for God** to give you opportunities to share your faith. You will be surprised how many chances you will have when you do this.

▶ **Rehearse your own** story of faith until you can share it without hesitation. Sharing your story may be the key to having a chance to pray with someone.

▶ **Follow up later** with the person you have prayed with. You will want to encourage them to find a fellowship and practice what they have professed.

> *It is not just human support, as important as that is, but our prayers that will bring powerful protection, strength, and results in our soul-winning efforts.*
>
> Evelyn Christenson

How do you keep praying when you know you will make mistakes?

The LORD directs the steps of the godly. He delights in every detail of their lives. Though they stumble, they will never fall, for the LORD holds them by the hand.

Psalm 37:23–24, NLT

76 question

How can you pray for someone who has hurt you?

Of all types of prayer, praying for someone who has hurt you can be the most challenging. A normal reaction to mistreatment is to defend yourself. And you certainly do not want to let yourself be taken advantage of again. But if you stay in that mind-set, you will not be able to obey God and pray for those who have mistreated you. If God tells you to pray for them, there must be a way to do it.

answer

You are not asked to pray for those who hurt you—you are commanded to. That is a tough admonition to follow. If God tells you to do something, He will give you what you need to do it. In order to pray for your enemies, you must come to a place of giving God your hurt and anger, and asking Him to replace it with His love. You cannot love your enemies in your own strength.

The parable of the unforgiving servant in Matthew 18 warns that God will not forgive you if you withhold forgiveness from others. Pray to be able to forgive, and be willing to pray for the offender as God leads, and He will give you the power to do it. It may seem to be too difficult when you begin to understand and practice this spiritual principle. It will become easier, however, as you enjoy the blessings of forgiveness. You may need to pray more than once before you can pray for others with the right attitude, but you need to go to God until you can.

There is such an urgency for this reaction of doing good in response to the evil done against you that the Bible says if you are coming to God and remember that you hold something against someone, you are to stop what you are doing and attend to that grudge immediately. Those feelings of unforgiveness and anger can stand between you and God and can affect your spiritual life.

worth thinking about

▶ **Finding a release** from and healing of wounds from the past may require additional help from a believing counselor or pastor.

▶ **Understand that the** feelings you experience are normal and should not cause you shame. Give yourself permission to have the feelings, and then let God take them.

▶ **Healing comes** in stages. Like any healing process, it will take time to be able to release your hurts and forgive.

> *Love your enemies, and be good to everyone who hates you. Ask God to bless anyone who curses you, and pray for everyone who is cruel to you.*
> Luke 6:27–28, CEV

question

Does it do any good to pray for the poor?

When you think of the poor, you can imagine an almost endless stream of people who live in poverty from all over the world. The vast dimension of the problem of the poor boggles your mind, and you cannot fathom that your prayers alone could make a difference. You feel that God wants you to pray for the poor, but your faith quavers at the thought, and you do not know where to begin.

answer

Understanding more of the character of God helps you understand the need and the requirement to pray for those who suffer from the indignity of poverty. God's word in the Bible admonishes, "If you see some brother or sister in need and have the means to do something about it but turn a cold shoulder and do nothing, what happens to God's love? It disappears. And you made it disappear" (1 John 3:17, THE MESSAGE). The love of God and His love of justice compel His actions toward those who have nothing. He asks that you pattern yourself after His character, and let yourself be transformed by His love into someone who can love this way.

If you love God, you love justice as well. If you love God, you love the poor and disenfranchised. If you love God, you know that His power is not limited, His will is perfect, and He sees each person and each person's needs. You are compelled to pray in faith and love for the poor. These parts of God's character are yours if you ask to be like Him. They will grow with time.

God promises that if His people will humble themselves, seek Him, and turn from their sins, He will forgive them and heal their land. You can cry out on behalf of those who have no voice and no hope, and you can be part of God's healing and provision. God is justice and mercy and love and compassion. Your prayers acknowledge who He is and ask Him to touch the lives of those who do not know those things.

worth thinking about

▶ The best place to be is resting in the knowledge that you have no idea how to solve a worldwide problem. That way, you go to God confident that He's the only One who knows what to do.

▶ No issue in the world is too big for one person to lift up in prayer. God hears each prayer, and His heart is already tender for the poor.

▶ Pray for the poor, but look for ways to help the poor in your area, and in the world. Prayer plus your actions equals powerful help for impoverished people.

▼

He who has mercy on the poor, happy is he.
Proverbs 14:21, NKJV

question

How should you pray for your children?

God said in the Bible that children are a blessing, but you may not feel that way every day. You know you need to pray for your children, but you are not sure where to start. You know there are scriptures that provide good instruction for your prayers, both for spiritual and physical things your children need, and for you to know how to parent your children. You want to know how to pray for them well.

answer

The Bible offers a wealth of wisdom on child rearing. Any aspect of your child's life, from healthy living to healthy morals, is covered in the Bible. The Book of Proverbs advises parents to train a child in how to live and gives the encouragement that as the child grows older, that training will come into play. Certainly the learning of God's truth must be the cornerstone for your child's development, along with learning to pray.

Realizing that God gave you your child and cares for that child more than you ever could care for him must prompt you to release his future to God. Pray for your child to accept a life of faith in God. Pray for his education, as well as for the spiritual education you provide.

Give God your concerns about the decisions your child makes and the friends he attracts. Pray for the health of your family and marriage, as these both affect your child. God will give you the wisdom to raise your child and to effectively deal with any problem that arises. Ask God to make you the parent He wants to raise the child He gave you. Share your prayers with your child, both to pattern the way you talk to God, and to let him know that you love him enough to bring his concerns to God, and he will feel cherished.

worth thinking about

▶ **Keep a list** of your current prayer focus for each child, and pray over it every day. Set a time for reviewing the list in prayer regularly.

▶ **Ask God** to direct you in decisions pertaining to activities, clubs, and lessons for your child. God will help you keep a balance in your lives.

▶ **Pray for the** child-care providers and teachers who care for your child. Pray for their wisdom and guidance when they are in charge of your child.

> *Lift up your heart to Him, sometimes even at your meals and when you are in company; the least little remembrance will always be acceptable to Him. You need not cry very loud; He is nearer to us than we are aware of.*
> Brother Lawrence

question

▼

Can you ask God to "fix" your spouse?

Keeping your marriage happy and healthy would be impossible without God's help. The world's stresses and temptations make any marriage a daily effort. You want to enlist God's help and pray for your spouse, but you want to know how to pray in the right way. You know what you want for your spouse, but you know it might not be what God wants.

answer

▼

The marriage relationship is complex, with emotions and in-laws and finances and children. Any two of those would be enough to strain a relationship, but with all the factors that two people bring to marriage, you need what God can provide to keep you happily married. When you pray for your spouse, you need to pray first that you are all that God intends as a partner for your spouse. Otherwise, you can easily fall prey to the temptation to tell God all the reasons He should "fix" your spouse.

Throughout the Bible, God gives you wisdom on love and marriage. He shows you the need for respect and love that holds no grudges and that does not count grievances. You are to put the other person first in your thoughts and actions, and treat your spouse as a gift from

God. You can pray each day for an aspect of your spouse's life—covering work relationships, finances, integrity in decisions, protection from temptation, and spiritual growth.

Ask God to unite the two of you spiritually, even as you unite physically. God's plan includes an order in the family based on relationship with Him. Ask Him to place you in His order and keep your family balanced. Pray together if you can, and pray for your children together. In all ways, try to "outlove" your spouse every day. Let God be your strength and love be your language.

worth thinking about

▶ The old adage to never go to bed angry is a good resolution to make. Agree to resolve any issues and pray before going to sleep, so slights cannot become larger.

▶ Resist the urge to share things about your spouse with others as prayer requests. Respect the privacy your family should enjoy.

▶ If communication is difficult or trouble arises, go to your pastor or trusted counselor for wisdom and prayer. Stop issues before they grow into troubles not easily fixed.

> *The most precious gift that marriage gave me was this constant impact of something very close and intimate yet all the time unmistakably other, resistant—in a word, real.*
>
> C. S. Lewis

question

▼

How can you pray for someone you don't know?

At some time, you will experience the strong desire to pray for someone you do not know. You may be shopping in a store, driving to work, or taking a walk, and suddenly someone catches your attention. You feel a strong urge to pray for him, but you are not sure what to pray. You know that God is asking you to pray, so you need to know how to find out what to pray.

answer

▼

If God moves you to pray for someone you do not know, He must have something in mind. You need to take a moment and ask God what to pray. You also need to ask God how to pray for this person—whether to pray right where you are or stop to speak to the person and ask if he or she would like you to pray for them. Praying for someone face-to-face takes more boldness, but God blesses you when you step out in faith.

Without a clear direction from God, pray for protection and God's blessings for the person's life. Pray that God's will is done and that the person's needs are met by His heavenly Father. God will cause the right words to come from your mouth, and whether the stranger responds to your prayer or not, you know that you have been obedient to the urging of God. The result is up to God.

Try to have a heart that beats like God's heart, and care about those who pass your way. If you stay sensitive to the small voice that tells you to stop and pray, you will also hear the promptings to share an encouraging word or compliment with someone, or to give something to someone in need. Prayer and acts work hand in hand to bless people for God.

worth thinking about

▶ **The Bible says** that you never know if you are extending kindness to an angel when you reach out to strangers. Treat each stranger you pray for as a treasured child of God.

▶ **If God prompts** you to offer practical help to a stranger, do not refuse. Whether the stranger accepts your help or not, you have given her a touch of God's love.

▶ **Fear of ridicule** or rejection can powerfully dissuade you from praying. Push through those feelings and obey what God has placed on your heart.

> *The LORD your God is the God of gods and Lord of lords. He is the great God, the mighty and awesome God, who shows no partiality and cannot be bribed. He ensures that orphans and widows receive justice. He shows love to the foreigners living among you and gives them food and clothing.*
> Deuteronomy 10:17–18, NLT

question

▼

Is it all right to ask for things?

When you enjoy a prayer relationship with God, you might find that you hesitate to ask for the things you need for fear of sounding greedy or selfish. There are times when you might even feel guilty asking for things when you know so many people around the world need so much more. You want to know if you can feel okay about asking God for what you need.

answer

▼

God lets you know many times through the words of the Bible that He will meet all your needs and that He cares for you. In the Book of Philippians, Paul wrote that you should be anxious for nothing, but with a thankful and confident heart, let God know what you need. He said that the result of approaching your needs with trust and without worry would be a heart full of God-given peace. God gives His permission and blessing on your requests for your needs. In the Lord's Prayer, one petition actually states, "Give us this day our daily bread (provision)." As the prayer model given by Jesus, you can understand that it really is permissible to ask God for what you need.

You must find a balance in the practice of asking God for things, though. A constant focus on your own needs can diminish the importance of your spiritual condition, and can dull you to the needs of others. Your choice of the things you believe you need also reflects your status with God on a spiritual level. The closer to God you become, the less focused you are on physical things.

Will a new car bring you peace or a deeper relationship with God? You may need a car for transportation, but if you ask God for a new sports car because you want to feel prosperous and successful, you will probably not receive that from God. Your identity and your self-image must be thoroughly grounded in God, and then you can trust that your requests will honor Him.

worth thinking about

▶ **Insecurity in God's** love can result in prayers that concentrate on the things that you can see and touch. As you grow, you will notice you ask for things less and less.

▶ **Ask God to** break your desire to accumulate things. Any habit can be broken and replaced by right desires through God's power.

▶ **Pray for a contented** spirit. God will cause you to be at peace with what you have, so you can be generous and free with your possessions.

> *When we humble ourselves like little children and put on no airs of self-sufficiency, but run happily into the joy of our Father's embrace, the glory of his grace is magnified and the longing of our soul is satisfied. Our interest and his glory are one.*
>
> John Piper

82 question

What is there to pray for besides your needs?

At times, prayer resembles a laundry list of needs and not much else. When you experience those times, it seems that your needs weigh so heavily on your mind that thinking of prayers for anything else is difficult. You know you need to pray for spiritual things for yourself and for others, but you do not know where to start. Spiritual things are hard to see and describe, but you know God has the answer.

answer

A very dynamic prayer recorded in the Book of Colossians for a group of people included hope that they would be "filled with the knowledge of His will in all wisdom and spiritual understanding," and that these friends would walk "worthy of the Lord, fully pleasing Him, being fruitful in every good work and increasing in the knowledge of God; strengthened with all might" (1:9–11, NKJV). That beautiful prayer touches on the vast nature of a relationship with God, and some of the needs that correspond.

The physical things you need in your life make up a very small part of your prayer relationship with God. What He desires is that you grow spiritually and continue to become closer to Him through your prayer and the reading of the Bible. He wants you to develop a hunger for more—more of God, and more of His ways.

The Bible is full of valuable things to think about, things good to desire and things beneficial to do. You can find inspiration for prayer on nearly every page of the Book: abundance, adventure, advice, alertness, appetite, aspirations are only the beginning of what God will help you with. The Bible is full of examples and motivation for everything that concerns you, and God will guide you. Praying for more love is wonderful. Praying to be contented with your life is great. Praying for peace and the ability to encourage other people is fantastic. If you ask God to let you know what you need in your life, He will lead you to the things best for you to pray.

worth thinking about

▶ **The one thing** God wants most from you in prayer is YOU.

▶ **It is wise** to seek the Giver, not the gifts. Focus on what you need to be closer to God, and your prayer will be a delight to God.

▶ **Spend time enjoying** God. This is a precious and valuable use of prayer and a way to balance out what you need with what will make you grow.

> God never gives us anything incidental. There is nothing easier than getting into the right relationship with God, unless it is not God you seek, but only what He can give you.
> Oswald Chambers

83 — question

Can you ask God for
your purpose in life?

A defining question throughout the ages has been
"What is the meaning of life?" Every person longs for
significance and wants to know that life has a purpose
beyond day-to-day schedules and details. When you
pray, you want to know if you can ask God if you have a
purpose, and ask for Him to show it to you, as well as
ask the reason for your life, or if those questions focus
too much on your own wants and desires.

answer

Realize God has a plan and a purpose for your life. He
said that He created you in intricate detail while you
were in your mother's womb, and that He knew every
day of your life before it even began. What amazing
thoughts! Even more amazing, the Book of Romans
states that God's Spirit prays for you, even as God works
all things for good for you as you remain devoted to
God, because you are called according to His purpose.

As long as you love God and obey what He tells you, you
can rest assured that your purpose is in progress. No surprise awaits you, because you will later find that you can
look back and see many ways God prepared you for your
purpose even when you were young. While a clear pic-

ture of your part in God's plan may not come right now, you can know He works all the time to prepare you.

Part of your purpose in life may involve some of the talents and abilities you know you have. You need to go to God and ask Him to refine those talents and abilities so they can be useful to Him. Be aware that attitudes of self-promotion or selfish purposes can stop God's plan for you. Ask Him to search your heart daily and show you any wrong thoughts. Any plan or purpose God assigns you is first and foremost for His glory. God's will stands at the heart of any purpose, and realizing you are just a part of that higher purpose will help keep your attitude one of thankfulness and humility.

worth thinking about

▶ What a curious tightrope you must walk, between rejoicing because you have a special purpose and remembering that you must yield to God's greatness and perfect will.

▶ If only to participate in the grand design of a prayer relationship, you have a great purpose in God's eyes.

▶ God will never call you to a purpose for which He has not already prepared you.

> We all have a specific task to do for God, and it was planned in His head before we were ever formed in the womb. That is an incredible truth.
>
> Marilyn Meberg

question

Should you bother God with small matters?

Most people want to pray when difficult situations arise or when they go through a crisis. Feeling overwhelmed brings a need to connect with God, who is bigger than any circumstance. But when no crisis comes, you find yourself wondering if you should bother God with the things in your life that annoy you, but are small compared to life-threatening illnesses and financial crises. If some concerns are too tiny to bring to God, you want to know what to do with them.

answer

People are split between two camps of thought when it comes to praying for the little things in life. Some think God should deal with only big items and disasters, because there are so many of those in the world at any given time. Others believe that God should get involved in just the things in life you cannot figure out. Both sides are wrong. No life of faith and prayer begins with the idea that anything limits God. He created everything, and He is infinite. His power knows no boundaries; nor does His concern for you.

Some people resist praying for small things because they think they will be bothering God. The Bible answers that concern when it states, "While they are still speaking, I will hear" (Isaiah 65:24, NKJV). Your God listens to you at every moment, and cares about your needs and concerns whenever He listens. If an issue is important to you, it is important to God.

Writer Amy Carmichael described God's intimacy in your life this way: "Our loving Lord is not just present, but nearer than thought can imagine—so near that a whisper can reach Him." Your relationship with God is close and intimate, and grows deeper over time. Concern about small things in your life should flow from your regular prayer conversations, just as other thoughts and feelings flow out to your Father's ear.

worth thinking about

- ▶ There are no small matters in the kingdom of God, only small prayers.

- ▶ If you could see how intricately God works all things for your good just because you love Him, you would never think that your concerns are too small for His attention.

- ▶ The Bible says to cast *all* your cares upon Him, just because He loves you. "All" means even the stubbed toe and the late mail and the car that will not start and the cat that ran away from home.

> It pleases [God] when we turn to Him in dependence and trust. When we ask in His Son's name, according to His character, God delights in proving His love, His wisdom, and His trustworthiness.
>
> Cynthia Heald

question

Can you pray to not go through hard times?

As your prayer life grows and matures, you find yourself facing the possibilities of difficult times. You want to ask God to let you avoid going through something hard, but you are not sure that you should. How can you let God know how much you do not want to go through something without telling Him you do not trust Him enough to believe you would be fine in the midst of it?

answer

Experiencing trials and troubles is not pleasant. Everyone faces difficulties at some point in their lives, and you are not alone in wishing you would not have to endure it. The Bible relates many stories of people who faced mean and impossible situations, and because trouble does not discriminate, those situations happened to good people and those who were evil alike.

When Jesus prayed to God the night before He was brutally crucified on the cross, He agonized over the sacrifice He knew He must make to redeem people from sin and death, but He still faced His strong desire to not go through it. He prayed that if there was any way to do things differently, He wanted to avoid it. He went on to pray, "Nevertheless not My will, but Yours, be done" (Luke

22:42, NKJV). Jesus modeled the perfect prayer when facing difficulties. He honestly shared His emotions with God and then yielded to God's perfect will for His life.

God does not waste one experience in your life. Even through the dark times and the hard trials you endure, God is creating in you stronger faith, deeper character, and understanding you would never gain without the troubles. The apostle Paul described being hard-pressed on every side yet not crushed; perplexed but not in despair; struck down but not destroyed; and yet always confident that God's highest purposes and strength would be manifested in his life. You can ask to avoid trouble, but ask God to do what is best in your circumstances.

worth thinking about

▶ Ask God to open your eyes to see what treasures He gives you during your trials.

▶ You would not purposely turn down a blessing from God. Be careful when you desire to avoid suffering. You may be refusing a blessing in disguise.

▶ The place your mind gives to suffering will determine how you respond to God. Realize that suffering is part of life, and you will look for what God has for you.

As a saint of God, my attitude toward sorrow and difficulty should not be to ask that they be prevented, but to ask that God protect me so that I may remain what He created me to be, in spite of all my fires of sorrow.
Oswald Chambers

How do you pray when you feel beaten down by life?

GOD holds the high center, he sees and sets the world's mess right. He decides what is right for us earthlings, gives people their just deserts. GOD's a safe-house for the battered, a sanctuary during bad times. The moment you arrive, you relax; you're never sorry you knocked.

Psalm 9:7–10, THE MESSAGE

86 question

▼

What do you pray when you aren't getting well?

Few things tax your patience and hope like suffering and lasting discomfort associated with an illness or injury. You know the Bible teaches you that God heals, and so you wonder if you have done something wrong that prevents God from healing your disease. Other people may even hint that you have too little faith to be healed, but you are not sure that is the answer.

answer

▼

God heals. Psalm 103 suggests that you purposely remember all God's benefits for you, including forgiveness from sins, God's kindness, His mercy, and the healing of all your diseases. The work done by Jesus when He gave up His life on the cross provided healing for all people so that death would no longer have an eternal grip. Healing can include healing of your physical body, healing of your mind and emotions, and any other healing you need.

Knowing all this, when you must endure a long-lasting illness, you find that your faith runs smack into your reality, and doubt enters your mind. If you have prayed for God to heal you, and He says He heals everything, then why are you still suffering? You want things to make sense, and it seems the only answer is that this situation makes little sense at all.

Take your doubt, frustration, and your pain to God. Talk to Him honestly and pour out your heart. Tell God that you realize He knows best. Tell Him that even as it makes no sense to you, you trust Him and believe that He has the situation under control and knows what you need. If you cannot pray that way, ask God for the faith to see things as He sees them. Healing may come, or healing in different parts of your life may come from enduring the illness. Either way, God is good and works all your circumstances for good in your life.

worth thinking about

▶ **You must be** convinced of the goodness of God. Any lingering doubt can grow in the frustration of long-term sickness. Read the Bible and encourage yourself.

▶ **Ask God to lead** you to help if you need it. He may lead you to another doctor or a different type of care. Let God lead.

▶ **Ask to be able** to rejoice in sufferings, and realize that your experience is not unique. Find the blessing that is always to be found.

> *It is the infinite, overflowing, swelling impulse of the Divine nature to cure souls of their diseases as the most adequate and normal of all the pacifiers of the mind and calmers of the nerves.*
>
> Joyce Meyer

87

Is it all right to ask God to change your traits or habits?

Seeing a need for change in other people is always easier than seeing a need for change in yourself. Negative traits in others are glaringly obvious and much clearer than your own negative traits. You know chances are you need to change, but you do not know exactly what you should ask. How do you know what to ask God and what changes you need?

answer

At times, you know what traits or habits in your life need to change. You may struggle with a bad habit that needs to be broken, or behavior toward people in your workplace or at home that you realize should be better. You can speak to God openly and honestly and ask Him to forgive you for your addiction to something or for your inconsiderate behavior. Ask God to change you. He may lead you to resources you need, or He may change something inside you that will cause you to lose your desire for the bad habit or behavior.

Certain parts of your life that function poorly may frustrate you, but you may not know the cause. It may be a struggle with the fear of trusting others, or anger that erupts every time you drive, or endless other possibilities.

You actually do not need to know the cause to be able to come to God and ask for help. Your confession of the problem, as well as your helplessness to control the problem, positions you to trust God for the change. He works according to the unique characteristics inherent in people and tracks healing and change in the way He knows is best for each person.

You will always be thoroughly human and in relationship with God on a spiritual basis. You will fall into sins and errors, and those sins and errors left untended can create a distance between you and God without your knowledge. It is a great idea to ask God every time you pray to show you anything that distances you from Him, so you can be free.

worth thinking about

- ▶ **A trusted friend** might be able to see what you should pray for yourself better than you can.

- ▶ **Keep God first**, and always thank Him for the life He's given you. If you concentrate too much on yourself, your point of view may become skewed.

- ▶ **Let God show** you how to change your habits and traits that need improvement.

> *Carefully build yourselves up in this most holy faith by praying in the Holy Spirit, staying right at the center of God's love, keeping your arms open and outstretched, ready for the mercy of our Master, Jesus Christ. This is the unending life, the real life!*
>
> Jude 20–21, THE MESSAGE

88

question

▼

Is it enough to ask only once for forgiveness?

When you think about asking forgiveness from God, it is hard to imagine that just asking once clears away your offense. You think of the number of times you have fallen back into something you already confessed to God, and the issue of forgiveness seems more complicated. You want to be sure you have prayed enough when you have sinned, but you also do not want to feel compelled to pray again and again for the same offense.

answer

▼

The beauty of an established relationship with God is that you can go to Him in confession and prayer, and know that your offense has been cast as far away as the east is from the west. That would be as far as you could imagine, and then even farther. When you confess your sin, God does not remember it unless you bring it up to Him again.

In this sense, you only have to ask Him once.

If you fall into the same sin again, you need to confess it to God again. Your first confession did not excuse the whole category of sin, just your episode of sin. As a matter of fact, if you find that you keep falling into the same sin over and over, you need to ask God to show you what you need to do to be free. That is a trap for you for some reason, and you need to watch and pray to escape its hold.

When you first go to God to establish and receive a relationship with Him, you confess that you know you are a sinner, and that only the sacrifice of Jesus and the love of God set you free from the destruction sin would bring. That confession establishes your relationship with God, but does not cover future sin. You need to keep coming to God daily and asking Him to examine your heart and your life, and show you any hidden sins or wrong motivations. You cannot know yourself that well, and by His grace, each time you go to Him, He forgives and heals you.

worth thinking about

▶ There is no fear in asking forgiveness from God. He freely gives it to you, with no strings attached.

▶ Actively examining yourself and your thoughts shows God you want to stay clear of sins that would cause distance between you. Cooperate with Him in confessing what He brings to your attention.

▶ God's forgiveness comes with more love and grace than you can even take in. Remember that when you need to forgive others.

> *Our holiness does not depend ever on what we do, but securely rests on God's shoulders. With that, we are not condemned when we fail and fall short, but rather we can press on toward the righteous life we were called to live.*
>
> Tracey D. Lawrence

89

question

How do you pray when it is hard to forgive?

Wounds of the heart from the actions of another run deep, and the emotions involved are complex. You can carry the pain in your heart from mistreatment for many years, and it can seem as fresh an injury now as it did in the beginning. You know God requires that you extend forgiveness, but when the pain is great, that forgiveness does not come easily. You need to know how to pray about the problem.

answer

Pouring your heart out to God starts the healing process. God will not flinch or turn away as you tell Him of your grief, or even when you overflow with bitterness. He created your emotions. He understands how people hurt other people, and even why it is so difficult to release those hurts. However, God still asks you to extend forgiveness to the one who hurt you as freely as you have received forgiveness from Him for your own sins.

Even with this understanding, you still face the problem of actually being able to forgive a person in the wake of great heartache. Even though the offense toward you may have been terrible, God would never ask you to do something this difficult without giving you what it takes to do it.

Going to God with a willing heart to forgive sets in motion the power you need to step aside from the pain and to release the offender. In the measure you can release someone to God, in that same measure you allow God to work on both sides of the issue. God honors the prayer that asks Him to make you *willing* to forgive. God will move you deeper into your own healing and will give you the power to release the pain. This may happen in prayer, or it may happen in counsel with someone. Your perspective will change the more you think about the free flow of God's mercy in your own life, even when you were not following God.

worth thinking about

- ▶ Know that praying more than once to reach a place of forgiveness is absolutely normal. Forgiveness is a process.

- ▶ Watch that your thoughts do not continually rest on the wrongs done to you. That will keep the bitterness alive and well.

- ▶ When you reach a place of forgiveness, ask God if you need to speak to the person you have forgiven, or if the matter is settled.

> *Let us lay aside every weight, and the sin which so easily ensnares us, and let us run with endurance the race that is set before us.*
> Hebrews 12:1, NKJV

question

▾

How can you pray for someone you don't like?

Praying for someone you enjoy comes easily. You can think of many blessings you would like to see God bring into that person's life. But praying for someone difficult or troublesome in your life poses a challenge. You do not want to pray with a bad attitude or simply avoid praying for that challenging person if you know that God is prodding you to lift the person up to Him in prayer.

answer

▾

God knows how complex human interactions can be. Feelings are hurt, bad memories linger, and at times people just cannot get along. God created people with emotions, so He understands, but He also understands that the reason for the problems is not just emotional vulnerability. People choose to do wrong things, and those wrong things can include hurting others. Your problem arises when you feel a burden or a strong reminder from God to pray for someone difficult who has hurt your feelings or been unpleasant to you.

You must fight the urge to pray for God to give the person what he deserves. You might have offended someone else in just the same way. Praying with a neutral attitude is key because having a preconceived idea of what God should do prevents the outcome from resting in His hands. If you find it hard to be neutral on the subject, ask God to help you. Let Him lead you through your emotions and hurts so you can pray objectively.

You can also simply pray that God's will be done in the person's life. God's perfect will extends to everyone, and to ask Him to have His way would usher that perfect will into your challenging person's life. Ask God to give His unconditional love to the person and heal the wounds behind the difficult behavior. If you struggle to view the troublesome person with God's eyes, ask Him to change your vision. Ask Him to give you His supernatural and unconditional love for the person and show you if an action from you might help deliver that message. Praying with an open heart can change your whole attitude.

worth thinking about

▶ **You need to keep** in mind that your concerns are not overlooked by God. Your responsibility is to pray when God prompts you.

▶ **The Book of 1 Peter** advises leaving room for the wrath of God. A gentler way to state that is: you pray, and God deals with the person.

▶ **Hurtful people** have usually suffered hurt themselves.

> *Teach us to fix our thoughts on you, reverently and with love, so that our prayers are not in vain, but are acceptable to you, now and always, through Jesus Christ our Lord.*
> Jane Austin

question

What do you pray when you do not need anything?

Far from being a complaint, the problem with having no currently unmet needs in your life is that you may feel stuck in your prayer life. When you begin to pray, many of your prayers revolve around the list of things you need. As you reach different stages of your life, your needs diminish, and then you wonder what to talk to God about when you pray. There has to be more to talk about than a list of wants.

answer

Much of your relationship with God eventually lies in worship—pure adoration and respect for who God is and what He means to you. In order for prayer to become its potential life-changing connection to the living God, as much time must be spent simply adoring God as is spent asking Him to meet your needs. You do need food to eat, a job for income, and all the essentials, but God needs your worship. While difficult to imagine, God, who needs nothing, wants your adoration. A parent basks in the moments when a son or daughter runs up just to hug and say "I love you!" Those rare and tender moments do more to bond parents and children than all the times the child asks for things. In a very similar way, God basks in your adoration and He soaks in your honor and praise.

Giving thanks for the blessings of God that leave you with no lack is a valuable prayer. God must be thanked when He provides for your needs. You can also pray for people around you who have needs. Your prayers are precious treasures.

For yourself, you can pray for greater spiritual maturity. That prayer pleases God. Scriptures in the Book of Ephesians record a prayer that asks that the eyes of your understanding be enlightened so you understand clearly the vast hope and promise of your relationship with God, and the greatness of His power. You always need maturity and deeper understanding of the marvels and complexity of God, so it is a prayer that is always appropriate.

worth thinking about

▶ **Time spent with** God is never wasted. By loving Him and worshiping Him, you can gain deeper faith and trust.

▶ **God has so** much more for you in prayer than you could ever imagine. Prayer is much more than asking and receiving.

▶ **Learn to enjoy** the company of God. He enjoys your company.

> *Do not have your concert first, then tune your instrument afterwards. Begin the day with the Word of God and prayer, and get first of all in harmony with Him.*
>
> J. Hudson Taylor

92

question
▼
How can anyone pray continually?

In the Bible, God asks believers to pray without ceasing, but that seems an impossible task. As much as you want to do what God said, many times just remembering to pray every day takes monumental effort, so the thought of trying to pray more seems inconceivable. How is it even possible for you to pray continually without neglecting your work, the care of your children, and the tasks that fill your day?

answer
▼

The Bible does say to pray without ceasing, but the same verse also directs you to be joyful always and to give thanks in everything. While the goal of continual prayer is requested, it involves more than simply petitioning God every hour of the day. The other two requests contained in the same verse describe a frame of mind rather than a direct action. To be joyful and thankful refers to adopting an outlook of happiness and gratitude based on the faithfulness of God's love and care.

In the same way, praying without ceasing means to go through your day with an attitude of connectedness to God, recognizing that He leads your steps during the day and that He continually provides what you need, day in and day out. Awareness of God effectively keeps the channel of prayer open. The experience of frequently enjoying God's presence, even in small moments in your day, honors Him.

Starting your day by acknowledging God and His rule in your life sets the tone for praying continually. Just as choosing to be happy and choosing to be thankful set a tone for your outlook to see the upside of life, determining to be aware of God throughout your day primes you to enjoy His presence and rest, knowing that He is in control of everything that happens to you. By keeping the lines of communication open, you can revel in the comfort that God is literally as near as your own breath.

worth thinking about

▶ **Some compare** continual prayer to sharing the same breath as God. Simple awareness of God's closeness throughout the day is prayer.

▶ **Remember that** your prayer life grows and changes over time. If you desire continual prayer, God will lead you there.

▶ **If God is** so close that He is in the office or car with you, your day may look quite different.

> *This is what it means to pray without ceasing. Not to always be speaking words, but to live in a state of spiritual receptivity, always having Christ's life flowing through you. His heart beating in you.*
>
> Jennifer Kennedy Dean

question

Should you have high expectations of God in prayer?

If you prayed to God but did not truly believe He could do what you asked, prayer would be a waste of time. Equally strange would be praying as an adult with a childlike image of God as a divine Santa Claus or magic genie. Your expectation of God and His power requires a balance between the two images, but you are not sure where to place your trust. You want to know how much to expect from God.

answer

You should have high expectations of God. Nothing anywhere compares to the magnitude of God. He cannot be explained or defined, and He knows no limits. A devotion to God in which you stand awed by His greatness pleases Him. As you grow closer to God and learn more about Him, your prayers will include more time spent adoring Him for who He is.

Out of that relationship of wonder and amazement, your faith will automatically increase. You cannot spend time thinking about God's power and love without your faith in His goodness increasing exponentially. Reading and studying the Bible also causes your faith in God to grow in great measure. Greater faith leads to greater expectations of God's power in answer to prayer. You can bring any kind of concern to God and have confidence that He will take care of it.

Recognizing God's limitless abilities when you pray is good. Applying that faith and expectation to demand specific answers from God is not good. Unless you strongly believe that God told you what answer to expect when you pray about a situation, you need to expect that God will answer your prayers marvelously, and thank Him in advance for all that He has done for you. Knowing what a great God you serve lets you know He will provide for you better than you could ever provide for yourself.

worth thinking about

▶ **Your expectation** and readiness to act on God's answers set the tone for your faith. Expect Him to answer and be ready if He asks you to act.

▶ **To stand in** prayer is a more powerful position than you will ever know. When you pray, you agree with what God is doing, and you ask Him to intervene in situations.

▶ **God's power** and His ability to provide for your needs are greater than you could even imagine.

> *I pray that Christ Jesus and the church will forever bring praise to God. His power at work in us can do far more than we dare ask or imagine.*
> Ephesians 3:20–21, CEV

question

▼

Does it matter if you are doing what God wants?

Because prayer centers on communication in your relationship with God, you question whether your behavior has anything to do with the success or ineffectiveness of your prayer life. The two ideas—your prayers, and your behavior the rest of the time—seem unconnected. You know that God looks at your heart and knows even your thoughts, so chances are your behavior matters to God when you pray, but it helps to know just how it matters.

answer

▼

The heart of your relationship with God depends on how you view God. If you see God as the One who, through His incredible love for you and His great mercy, reached down from heaven and made a way for you to have eternal life and be set free from the traps of the devil, then you will want to please God in your prayer life and in your behavior every day. Your gratitude for His love will compel you to want something better to give to Him in return.

If you have not reached a point where you can connect with the unfathomable grace of God, spend more time talking to God and invest more time in reading God's words so the vastness of God becomes as much a part of your consciousness as the workplace where you spend your days. God does not condemn you if you have not yet reached that point. He says, "Call to me and I will answer you. I'll tell you marvelous and wondrous things that you could never figure out on your own" (Jeremiah 33:3, The Message).

Understand, though, that because of Jesus, the line in the sand was drawn forever. God even called the workers of the devil "sons of disobedience" (Colossians 3:6, NKJV), stating that because of Jesus, you are separated forever from those sons of disobedience and all their evil works and desires, and you are part of God's kingdom—a trophy of His grace and His workmanship. God provided the way so that you could be free from the compulsion to be disobedient. In recognition and gratitude for that gift, you must embrace your freedom and walk in a way that is pleasing to God.

worth thinking about

- ▶ **Any prayer starts** best by asking God for a clean heart and forgiveness. This willingness to be obedient pleases God.

- ▶ **What God wants** most is your heart in a relationship of prayer. When you are praying sincerely and regularly, it should be easier to obey in other ways.

- ▶ **Always realize** the frailty of the human heart, and your proclivity to err. That way you will ask God for help every day.

> *Things right in themselves may become wrong things when they are allowed to fasten themselves excessively upon our hearts.*
>
> E. M. Bounds

95 | question

How does the Holy Spirit help you pray?

All believers have the Holy Spirit in their lives as comforter and teacher. Jesus told His disciples that when He went back to heaven, He would leave the Holy Spirit to help His people until Jesus returned. The Bible says that the Holy Spirit helps you pray when you cannot find the words, but what exactly does that mean?

answer

How loving and marvelous is a God who not only establishes prayer as a means of constant communication available to believers, but who also provides the backup for times when the burden of prayer weighs too heavy for words to describe! The Bible says that when you get tired in the waiting, the Holy Spirit prays in and for you. This is a constant action for you under God's direction.

This loving action of the Holy Spirit bolsters you when you are at a loss for words. When it's difficult to know what to say and what to pray, when the right words escape you, the Holy Spirit will pray alongside you with deep sighs.

This ministry of intercession by God's Spirit enables you to know that even if you forget to pray about some things, or do not understand a situation well enough to know how to pray, you are covered. The Holy Spirit intercedes on your behalf. Great relief comes in knowing that when you are undone by stress and grief, and tears are the only expression you can utter in prayer, the Holy Spirit knows precisely what prayers need to be lifted up and does that for you. This incredible blessing is yours because of the love of the Father.

worth thinking about

▶ **When you cannot** put your prayers into words, God hears your heart.

▶ **No more beautiful** thought exists than the Holy Spirit gathering your groans of prayers beyond words, and forming them into prayers to God. God honors those prayers.

▶ **God cares enough** even to remove the fears of inadequacy in His presence. You know that the Holy Spirit is always there as a go-between or to pray. You are never alone.

> We may not know how to word our prayers. We may find ourselves too weakened by grief or depression or failure to verbalize a prayer. But the promise of the Lord is that He takes even these glances and groans toward Him and makes them into effective pleas for help and mercy.
>
> William P. Barker

What do you do with your anger when you pray?

The LORD will answer when I call to him. Don't sin by letting anger control you. Think about it overnight and remain silent. Offer sacrifices in the right spirit, and trust the LORD.

Psalm 4:3–5, NLT

Does fasting make prayer more effective?

Many verses in the Bible reference fasting as an extension of deeper prayer or an expression of grief, sorrow, or repentance in prayer. Jesus taught His disciples how to behave *when* they fasted, not *if* they fasted. Fasting as a discipline of a lifestyle of prayer seemed expected, but that teaching is not common today. If believers fasted then, you want to know if fasting in conjunction with prayer would benefit you now.

answer

In any act of self-discipline in your spiritual life, there is danger of taking on the belief that if you do one thing, God will respond by doing another. God does not bargain, nor does He give away His favors to good little children. The heart of prayer is communion with a Holy God, and that communion requires a continually growing understanding of God's perfect will and rightness in all He does.

In the Psalms, fasting and prayer express great humility or sorrow to God, and include heart cries for His mercy and grace. Jesus fasted for forty days in the desert before starting His public ministry, and He turned every one of the devil's temptations back on him during that time.

Moderation, self-denial, prayer, and fasting fortify the heart for prayer.

If you make a decision to fast, you must look at it as not just a practice of denying yourself food, but also as a way to remove simple pleasures from your life for a time, and devote your attention during the fast to praying and studying the Bible more fervently than before. By making your own will bow to God's will for a time, your prayer life will grow and your faith will increase. In this way your prayers become more effective.

Only with God are you strong when you are weak. God's strength meets your weakness in fasting.

worth thinking about

- ▶ **If a practice** draws you closer to God, then it has merit. If it does not, it is wasted effort.

- ▶ **Fasting or any** other discipline, done in your own strength, will not make your prayers more effective.

- ▶ **Only when you** rely on God for the strength to proceed will you see the increase in power.

> *Fasting confirms our utter dependence upon God by finding in him a source of sustenance beyond food. Through it, we learn by experience that God's word to us is a life substance, that it is not food ("bread") alone that gives life, but also the words that proceed from the mouth of God (Matthew 4:4).*
>
> Dallas Willard

question

▼

How do you keep from getting discouraged?

Discouragement comes quickly when answers to prayer come slowly, or when your circumstances seem larger than life. You start to wonder if God plans to help you in your troubles. At first, nagging doubts play in your mind, and then full-blown discouragement moves in, and before you know it, hope and trust in God are spread thinner and thinner. The progression into discouragement happens so quickly that it is hard to imagine how to stop it.

answer

▼

The life of a believer always goes through low places and high spots. During the high spots, you see God working in obvious ways, and you feel that no enemy could bring you down because your God protects and blesses you. But in the low places, where help seems to come at the last minute and you wish you had blessings of any kind, you fall prey to the temptation to lose all hope.

God never plays with believers, changing things to keep them on their toes. He does allow certain things into your life at certain times to stretch your faith and force you to exercise your self-control. Difficult times test your resolve to believe in God despite the circumstances.

A way to prevent discouragement comes from the Book of Hebrews. There you will find that the prescription for hopelessness is to take time to remind yourself of all that Jesus endured for you in order to give you the irrevocable hope of eternal life. Reminding yourself of the magnificent grace of God that brought you into His forever family puts all trouble in perspective. Recalling answers to prayers in the past helps you remember that God always comes through. And reading God's words in the Bible infuses you with faith-building encouragement.

worth thinking about

▶ Discouragement comes when your focus is on the size of the problem and not on the size of God.

▶ Spending time in fellowship with other believers can keep your faith levels high and give you encouragement to believe.

▶ Praying, reading books by godly authors, singing hymns or praise songs—all build you up and increase your hope and trust in God.

We may experience times of unusual closeness, when every prayer is answered in an obvious way and God seems intimate and caring. And we may also experience "fog times," when God stays silent, when nothing works according to formula and all the Bible's promises seem glaringly false. Fidelity involves learning to trust that, out beyond the perimeter of fog, God still reigns and has not abandoned us, no matter how it appears.

Philip Yancey

question

▼

What happens if you do not feel close to God?

You may believe that your best prayer times occur when you feel close to God. When that warm feeling is absent, you may avoid prayer altogether because it seems you are not connected to God enough to be heard. The Bible gives plenty of evidence that God is never far off, but feelings are real and hard to argue away. You want to know if you should pray when you feel far from God.

answer

▼

Truth from the Bible states that God always knows your thoughts and your concerns. He hears every prayer you utter, whether you are aware or not. God does not go away or move farther from people. He is at the helm of the universe every moment of every day. The reality is that distance from God can only exist because you have moved.

God beautifully laid out the way to return to closeness with Him in James 4:7, which says to give yourself to God and refuse to be swayed by the devil. He promises that if you say no to the devil, the devil will run from you. When you draw nearer to God, God comes nearer to you, but you have to watch out for and get rid of all sin that pesters you. Decide if you are going to go full bore for God, because you cannot follow God and the things of the world at the same time. He says, "Be happy!" for when you go to God humbly and without pride, He will make you greater.

God promises that if you draw close to Him, He will reward your effort with His closeness. All He asks is that you get rid of any sin that stands between you, and any affection for the ways of the world that keeps you from following God's ways. When you go to God and ask what He already wants to give, you will receive it. You can pray, even when you feel far away, as long as you are working to stay near to God.

worth thinking about

▶ **You cannot be** close to God if you allow other things to become priorities over Him. God will not compete for your affection.

▶ **Feelings must not** rule in spiritual matters. Your faith and the truth of God are your standard. Make decisions based on those things.

▶ **The more you** pray, the closer you get to God. It will take a lifetime to fully enjoy the presence of God.

I see true prayer, like all true obedience, as a constant struggle in which you make headway by effort against what opposes, and however much you progress you are always aware of imperfection, incompleteness, and how much further you have to go.

J. I. Packer

question

Does love have anything to do with prayer?

When defined as communication with God, or as an expression of your relationship with God, prayer sounds almost clinical and very practical. When you add love to the mix, the definition of prayer becomes more complicated. God is Love, and everything He does is motivated by love, so you know your prayer should reflect God's character as well, but you do not know what that would look like in your daily routine of a prayer life.

answer

No one can fathom the depth of love that drives God in all He does. He created the world and people to live in it just because He loves. He patiently waits to fulfill His perfect will out of love. He *is* Love, defined and infinite. Joining with God in the living relationship of prayer brings you into His existence of love.

You cannot experience the presence of God daily in prayer without your eventual transformation to His kind of supernatural love. Your understanding grows and you see His love behind every blessing and answered prayer. Your own motivations change as you see that God's admonition to love your neighbor as yourself is an act of obedience for you. Maturity causes you to see the folly of loving only when you want to.

The words in 1 Corinthians 13 beautifully describe what love means in your life. You see that even if you speak in the most eloquent of words, without love you might as well be a lot of noise and clanging. If you have much spiritual understanding and have great faith that can even move mountains, but have no love, you are nothing. Even the greatest sacrifice and deprivation will gain you nothing without love, for love is the fuel of God's power toward you. Love transforms prayer into a lifeline of hope. Love ignites your compassion for others and propels your giving. Love speaks God's language.

worth thinking about

▶ **Prayer makes** it possible to experience the love of God and to accept the gift of God in your life.

▶ **Becoming like Him** means becoming a carrier of love. Let yourself be filled with the love of God and spill out on the people around you.

▶ **Love powers God's** favor and blessing. Learn His language of love, and learn to share in His love action of blessing others.

> *Faithfulness to Jesus Christ is the supernatural work of redemption that has been performed in me by the Holy Spirit.*
> Oswald Chambers

100 question

What benefit comes from praying with others?

You understand that prayer is the lifeblood of your relationship with God, and you know that to keep your relationship healthy, you have to communicate with God every day. Much of the work and the privilege of prayer happens in your private time with God. But you want to know why God mentions the act of praying with other believers so many times, and what benefit comes from making the time to do that.

answer

The unity of believers merited special attention from Jesus. The last prayer He spoke while on earth that was recorded in the Bible asked God to make people one, as God and Jesus were One. He prayed that the divine agreement and oneness experienced with God would be the kind of unity people on earth would experience.

Believers are compared to parts of a body, with each part serving a different purpose, but making up a whole. Each person comes equipped with different gifts and abilities, and each person claims a unique personality. Together, those gifts, abilities, and personalities all work for the greater good God wants, by fitting together and working in the power of God.

When a group or community of believers pray and experience God's presence, transformation occurs both in the group and in the individuals within the group. There love can grow and lives can change more readily, for there is power in unity. Shared stories and encouragement flow in the atmosphere of a community. And the love of Jesus increases as the body of believers care for one another. And prayer finds its higher expression as each member of the community responds to God through his or her own unique understanding. Unity can only be achieved in a group of people with a common goal, and a praying group of believers will find that place.

worth thinking about

▶ **Fellowship with other** believers in prayer keeps you balanced and hones your ability to hear from God.

▶ **Praying with others** can teach you about prayer in ways that you could not learn alone.

▶ **God's purposes** and will are intertwined with believers willing to join together and pray in unity. By praying together, you are a part of fulfilling His purpose and will on earth.

Prayer is the strength of our individual and community existence. It is through prayer that we find the heart of our love relationship with Jesus as individuals, and it is through the love relationship of Jesus working in individual lives that communities prosper in peace and unity.

John Michael Talbot

Readers who enjoyed this book will also enjoy

100 Answers to 100 Questions About God

100 Answers to 100 Questions About God's Promises

100 Answers to 100 Questions About Loving Your Husband

100 Answers to 100 Questions About Loving Your Wife

100 Answers to 100 Questions to Ask Before You Say "I Do"